DEDICATION

To Lord, my God
and Father...

.

Paula Avila

Paula Avila

"Whatever comes, let it come. What stays let it stay, what goes, let it go."

Paula Avila

ACKNOWLEDGMENTS

It is my privilege to release the feelings of my gratitude to the people who helped me directly and indirectly in writing this lovely book.

I express my heart full indebtedness and owe a deep sense of gratitude to my husband Chris Avila for always supporting me and enjoying my dreams.

I am extremely thankful for my son Joao Avila for his dedication and support in helping me finalize this book.

I also thank my son Lucca Avila and my sister Roma Guizelini for always being there in this path of my life.

Thank you, Sean Jay Richardson and Elizabeth Smolinski, for working with me in pursuing . ʳ dream.

Issues

1 CHAPTER

I am very busy these days. Finishing my senior year of college has been quite stressful. Besides classes and schoolwork, I have all these interviews with law firms. My high GPA has attracted some attention from well-known corporations.

I am very proud of myself for almost completing this step in my professional life, but I will miss my friends and college life. When I finished high school, I was awarded many scholarships. My family and I are so grateful for this because it has allowed me to pursue a great career at a wonderful school. I have always wanted to be a lawyer, like my dad.

When I was little, I loved listening to my dad talk about his cases, the judges and everything.

Ever seen then, I was sure that I would be a lawyer one day, too.

My dad graduated from Harvard Law School, but I was not sure if I want to go to Harvard, Stanford or Yale.

After a long conversation with my parents, I decided to go to Harvard. My dad was so excited and proud of me that made me so happy and confident about my decision.

Now I am here, in my last year, finishing law school.

My college years were great, but I just studied. I never really partied or hung out with friends too much... I was always doing projects, studying, at the library and working as an intern in law offices.

I guess it's worth it. Today, I can choose where I want to work and I'll make a great deal of money. I could always work in my dad's office, but I really want to do my own thing. Unlike when I graduated high school and was choosing a college, I want to make this decision myself.

My dad is a very highly regarded lawyer in our town, Greenwich, Connecticut. My dad has worked for big corporations across the United States and sometimes in Europe. All his dedication and professionalism have made him a very rich man.

Also, he is a good investor. He owns a lot of properties. My brother and I were very lucky kids. My mom was always a stay-at-home-mom and gave us all the support that we needed to prosper academically. My brother, Robert, is also a lawyer and he works with my dad. Robert has the same dedication and professionalism my dad has.

Tonight, after all these years, I will go out to a party... People always called me a nerd, but tonight, I want to enjoy myself at the club. After all these years of college, I deserve it... If I even know how to party, I guess...

I bought a black dress for tonight and it looks beautiful on me! I love it! My friend Emma is coming with me... We are both so excited to go out.

"Sophie, what time are we going?"

"Around ten o'clock, I guess..."

"So, Sophie, I will finish that book I told you about and I will stop by, ok?

"Emma, are you going to do your hair? "

"I guess so Sophie, but I'd rather be reading this than doing my hair"

"I agree with you, Emma, but I am going to start doing mine right now. I heard Jerry is going tonight."

"Oh, really? He is such a weird guy, Sophie."

"Emma, we are weird too, and plus, I think he is hot… Tonight, I want to have fun."

"Did you finish your project for Dr. Carson's class?"

"Yes, Emma, I finished yesterday."

"Ok, see you at ten o'clock tonight."

"Ok, see you."

Emma is worse than me… She just loves books. She never even pays attention to guys. She is a very dedicated student.

Jerry is my classmate. He is very polite and a great student. His GPA is almost a 4.0. He is incredibly smart. He comes from a line of very powerful lawyers in San Francisco.

Jerry and I met when we got paired to do a semester long group project one time. We spent almost five months together to finish it. The objective was to defend a client who committed a tax fraud in NY. To complete this project with Jerry and I's high standards, we had to work super late nights especially because of all the other classes, studying, and projects we had on our plates.

Spending so much time with Jerry made me

feel comfortable enough to ask him if he is going out tonight. He just answered: "Yes, I'm going!"

I can't tell if he likes me or not… or if he just wants to be friends.

One night, when we were working, Jerry went to the next room and grabbed a bottle of wine. In the doorway, he popped the cork:

"Let's relax and think more clearly!"

"Of course, Mr. Jerry!" I said.

We drank and talked… Jerry and I laughed much more than you'd imagined. I was a little drunk. Looking at him, I wanted to kiss him so bad… The occasion was so perfect: wine, laugher and Jerry, handsome as ever, right in front of me. Alas, nothing happened that night. This happened over two years ago. I hope tonight my dream can come true.

Emma just got to my apartment. We must go soon:

"Wow, Sophie! You look so beautiful! I've never seen you dress up like that!"

"Thank you, Emma, you look beautiful too.

Emma and I got at the club around eleven o'clock at night. Inside was crazy: loud music, people screaming and a lot of people looking to have a good time. I guess my chance of bumping into Jerry will be close to zero. This place is so crowded… OMG!

Emma and I went to the bar. I asked for one Martini and Emma asked for a coke:

"Really Emma? Coke?

"Why not? I don't drink alcohol…" You know that. I will be fine with coke."

"All right, I don't drink that much, but today is a special occasion… Have you seen Jerry around?"

"It's impossible to find someone in this messy place. Sophie, those people are crazy!"

I laughed at Emma's face. She was shocked because people were jumping, dancing, and singing. My guess is she will leave soon. Anyway, I need to find Jerry…

"Sophie, I don't think that Jerry will be here. He isn't the type of guy to be at a club like this."

"I agree with you Emma, but let's go around for a little bit, at least… Maybe we can find him."

"Well I would go, if we could move from this spot…"

So, Emma was right, the club was too full and we are not used to it... I felt like this place was not for us. So, we left the club around eleven forty-five.

We went back to our dorms... When Emma said:

"Let's finish that book, Sophie?"

"I guess this is my life... I just don't understand why Jerry did not show up."

"Maybe he went, but like me, he did not see anything but a very dark, loud scary place."

"Come on Emma! It was not that bad."

We were kept talking till we got to my room. By the hallway, Emma and I saw someone set down in front of my room. We look at each other and I try to guess who was there... maybe Jerry... I cannot see that far, but my wish was him there.

"Sophie, who is this guy?"

"I think is Jerry."

"He has flower in his hands."

"Emma, I don't know."

We keep walking to get in my room, and closer we get there I was pretty sure that was not Jerry... I was so sad

"Hey girls!"

"Hi Carl."

"Hello Carl, what you are doing here?" Said Emma.

"Hi Sophie, I was thinking if we can go out for a little bit?

"I guess she cannot, we have a book to finish tonight." Said Emma.

"Hi Carl." I said. "Wait Emma, we can finish the book tomorrow."

"Those flowers are for you Sophie."

"Thank you, Carl."

"So, Sophie, I guess that I will finish the book, see you tomorrow."

"See you Emma."

So, I don't know why Carl is here and it was a surprise. We never talked that much and we just have some class together. I accept the flowers. We went to my room and I put the flowers in the jar. He is the type of guy that is quieter, very responsible and a great student. But he is not a type the guy that I like. But we can talk at least.

"So, Carl, did you go to the club tonight?"

"Oh no Sophie! I don't like places like that. There Too many people and the music is way too loud, on top of the absurd prices of everything"

"I couldn't agree more… Emma and I went there for a little bit and we felt like we were outside of the box"

"Sophie, there is a bar nearby. Do you want to go and have a drink? Maybe eat something?

"Sure, why not?"

When we were leaving the dormitory, I saw Jerry come from the library. I cannot believe he was in the library tonight!

He is coming in our direction… my heart beating faster and faster and I don't know what to do…

"Hi Sophie, Hi Carl."

"Hello Jerry!" Said Carl.

"Did you come from the library?" I asked.

"Yes, Sophie… I needed to finish some projects and when I saw the time it was too late. Where you guys going?

"I don't know, Carl invited to go to the bar. My guess it is close here. Am I right Carl?"

"Yes, I invited her to go with me at The

Sinclair"

"Wow, it is a nice place! Enjoy guys!"

"Thank you, Jerry." I said.

I was waiting for Jerry all night and he just passed by me… Why did I want to go with Carl to this bar?

"Carl? Sorry, but I think I am not feeling well…"

"Really? Are you ok?"

"No, I am not feeling well. I want to go back to the dormitory"

"Sure, Sophie."

I am sorry Carl. I don't want to go out with you. But I cannot say it to you. You are a nice guy and I don't want to hurt you. So, I need to say that I am sick.

Carl was very nice and left me in my apartment:

"I hope you feel well Sophie."

"Thank you, Carl."

Probably, if I did not see Jerry, I would have enjoyed talking to Carl. But, seeing Jerry made my heart beat more than I can imagine. I don't want to spend time with Carl, thinking and thinking why Jerry did not show up at the club.

I really wish today I had kissed Jerry, drank with him and maybe slept with him. I just have a couple days left at college and I want to spend time with Jerry.

I laid down on the bed and I put my headphones on… The song Issues played on my phone. I love this song. When I hear this song, my stomach hurts a little bit and I really want to kiss Jerry, but it is just feelings. It is better I come back to the real world: finish the book!

I took out the heads phones and got my book to enjoy it.

2 CHAPTER

I wake up the next morning with my cell phone ringing. It was my dad.

"Hi dad."

"Hi Sophie, I was talking with Professor Williams about your GPA and he told me that you will finish college with a great result. I am so proud of you Sophie!"

"Yes dad, I was working hard all those years…"

"I believe it Sophie!! So, when you come home?"

"In a couple days dad, I guess on Friday I

will be free."

"Great!"

"Ok dad, thank you for calling me"

"You're welcome Sophie, I love you!"

"I love you too dad, tell Mom I love her too"

"Ok, I will tell her"

OMG, I am so tired! At least I finished the book. I must shower and I need to go to the office, that I worked, to take my stuff.

My dad is very excited because I finish law school. He is thinking that I will work for him or maybe we will open our office together. But it will not happen. I already accepted an interview in NY. I want to work in one big company to get more experience in my career. Dad is an excellent professional, but now I want to decide my future. Sorry dad!

Why did I not see Jerry last night? I was trying so hard to find him. Sucks… I will leave this college without a date. Nerd girl!

I met with Emma at Professor William's office to hand in our last project. Emma asked me how my night with Carl was.

"I went back to the apartment; I was not

feeling well enough to go out." I said

She looked at my face and said, "I cannot believe you Sophie!" So, we gave to the professor our projects and when we were leaving the office, he called me back. At first, I thought I did something bad or my project was wrong, I don't know...

"Sophie, I saw that you receive a lot invitation for work?"

"Yes, professor William, I did receive a lot."

"Did you accept one yet?"

"No professor William, not yet."

"If you want, I have an office in London and China. If you are interested to talk about it, I am available."

"I am very honored to hear that! Thank you very much Professor William! I have an interview in NY, it is a great company that I dreamed of working there. But I promise that I will think about it"

"Of course, Sophie! Follow your dream! I just offer in case that one day you be interested on it"

"Really appreciate it Professor William."

I felt so happy for the Professor William invitation. He is one of the best professors in

Harvard Law School. Even if he just talks to me, it will make me very proud of myself.

"What did he say to you Sophie?"

Emma asked me very surprise, Professor Williams never talk with a student personality. Always talk to students in group.

"Nothing special! He just said good luck to me".

"Hum, I don't believe Sophie, but if you don't want to say, I respect it"

"Thank you, Emma. Let's go to lunch?"

"Sure. Let's enjoy this campus, we just have a couple days left. When do you leave Sophie?"

"I leave Friday."

"Really? I hope we can be in contact Sophie; I will miss you!"

"Definitely Emma. We were together for at least four years. I already miss you."

How nice is to have a friend like Emma? She is seriously a funny girl. I loved spending time with her doing homework, projects or even reading books. Emma is very smart and likes to question our opinions about certain cases in court. She is from Boston, Massachusetts. Her family is also in the law business. She will work with her dad in his office. She is very proud to work with him.

We had lunch together. We talked about our future careers and I told her that I will not work with my dad. She just said, "Enjoy your decision". I just laugh and for a second I stop and look around me: this University made me so happy and now I have to go home and bring with me all the memories: good and bad memories.

I will never forget my first day here. I felt so free and independent when I got there. Harvard is so fascinating. But now it is all done. I finish this chapter of my life. Now I am free to go and enjoy my career. Far away from here…

3 CHAPTER

Wow... how many bags did I bring? My dad and my brother come here to pick up. My mom probably stayed at home to organize a party for me. That's fine, but I wish when I got home, I could just relax. Emma was there to say goodbye. We hug each other. Emma was a great friend... We have each other for a long time. Great support Emma was for me.

"Sophie, we are done with your bags..."

"Sure dad. Thank you. I am ready to go. Bye Emma, I hope I can see soon."

"Bye my best and only friend that I have. By the way, your brother is so hot... Why have you never told me about him?"

"He is boring, trust me…" and I winked.

We laughed… we hugged each other for the last time and I got in the car. The car drove slowly and I had a chance to see this beautiful place for the last time, I guess…

It was very busy leaving Boston, but after 45 minutes we took the 95 South.

My dad struck up a conversation; "So, Sophie, how are you feeling? Leaving college and all of your friends behind, it must be a pretty significant change"

"I'm ok… I'm ready to leave it all behind, the past is the past, I'm just ready for my next step" I responded.

He jumped "Your next step? I thought it was going to be *our next step*. I sure hope you're talking about our new office?"

I hesitated for a moment, "Dad… I want to work in New York."

My dad shocked, and a little disappointed, only reply's with:

"Are you sure Sophie?"

"Yes dad, I am certain."

He was quiet for a few minutes, I could tell he

was upset. He was excited for us to work together, but in a low voice he said. "That's fine, I understand."

It turned awkward very fast and I wanted to change the conversation with my brother:

"So Bob, how is the office? Are you working hard?" I asked him.

"Yeah, it's really busy and we get a lot of clients. So where in New York do you want to work?".

He made it worse.

"Well… I have an interview next Tuesday. The office's name is Partner Group Financial Institution. It's in Manhattan."

"I know where that is. It's overlooking the Bryant Park and New York library, right?" My dad chimed in, I could tell he was still upset.

"Yes it's that one. The building name is W.R. Grace Building I believe."

"They are great company and have a lot of offices in The United States." Bob also commented.

We didn't talk that much; my dad was upset that I didn't want to work with him and my brother only made things worse. I was sorry, but I wanted to do my life how I wanted to.

It was the longest three hours ever. A long quiet moment, but at least I can appreciate the view of Connecticut. The trees and the green was so amazing. It was fantastic. Connecticut is a beautiful state. The nature is almost perfect. Looks like a picture drawn by an artist. Each tree has such a different green color. How it can be that amazing? It's   beautiful…

4 CHAPTER

We get home. I am tired and I guessed right, we have a party at my house. I see a lot of my parent's friends. My mom is the perfect hostess. There were a lot of white roses. My home is so cozy and beautiful.

My dad parked the car and my mom came running to us:

"Darling Sophie, how I missed you! Welcome back home baby!"

"Thank you, mom…"

"Everybody is here to celebrate you coming back home and guess who is here? Conner!"

"Mom stop! I need to take shower at least,

and Conner, Jesus Christ, mom. I don't like him, please."

So, anyways I went to greet everyone in the party, before I showered. It was fun seeing everybody again.   Conner come to talk to me. He was my boyfriend. We broke up years ago, but my mom wish we can come back together again. No way…

"Hi Sophie! How are you?"

"Hi Conner! I am fine, thanks."

"You look great, Sophie!"

"Thank you, Conner! You too…"

"Welcome home. Your mom was so excited about you return home."

"Yes, I can imagine… The party looks good, don't you think?"

"Oh yeah, it is. My parents are at that table let's go there to you said hi to them."

"Sure."

I think my mom will not be that excited when she realizes that I will be moving to NY.

I talk to Connor's parents and others of my parents' friends. Everyone was very kind and friendly with me. I excused myself from everyone and I went to take a shower.

When I went inside, I met Maria. Maria is a housemaid that work with my mom for decades. She knows me and my brother since we were kids. She loves us. Maria is a part of our family.

"Hola nina… Como estas?"

"Hola Maria…estoy bien."

"We missed you so much Sophie. We all are very happy that you're back home!"

We hug each other, and we always talk in Spanish to practice my Spanish. Maria bring me to my room and explain where everything is and if I need something let her know.

"Thank you, Maria, you are very sweet…"

"It is my pleasure Sophie."

My stomach get butterflies when I saw my old room. Living for this long time at the college, I can't imagine living here again. This room belonged to such a young girl and it was not me anymore. I want to move out. I can't come back to leave with my parents again. I need my space.

I sat down on the sofa that was in the corner of my room and many memories came to my mind. Also, times of confusion and scary thoughts of the future after school. Now, I am here and I laugh about everything that was in the past.

My bags were there, but I couldn't organize it then. Better I get this shower and come back to the party.

5 CHAPTER

After eating, drinking and talking, people start to leave the party. I set down with Connor and we started to remember old times.

"Do you remember our first kiss Sophie?"

"Yes, I do Connor… it was in this lake."

"I miss you Sophie. Now that are you coming back maybe we can try it again…we had a great relationship before you went to college…"

"Conner, I will not live here. I will be moving to New York, probably in two weeks."

"What? but your father commented that you and him, maybe your brother, will open a law office in Greenwich…? Did he know about your decision?"

"Yes, I told him today."

"Everyone expects that you will be here with your family, once your father has a great law office reputation…"

"Yes, I know it. But, for now I want to go on my own. I need and want to create my own career. I don't want to be like my brother."

"That's fine, and I'm guessing that we don't have any chance together?"

"No Conner, we don't…"

We keep talking about an hour. During our conversation I had time to appreciate the lake: the reflection of the moon in the water's lake was splendid. The moon was full and shine that made possible to see the side of the lake: I can even see the trees. What a beautiful image. It was a great time, but I don't love Conner. He is a gentleman but isn't the man I want for my life.

Conner talked about his office clients and how growing he is in his professional life.

"Sorry Conner, my friend Emma is calling me, just one second…"

"Sure Sophie!"

"Hey girl! How are you?

"Hi Sophie! I am fine and about you? Did you get home safe?

"Yes, Emma, I did…"

"Well, just wanted to say hello and ask when you are going to do the interview in NY?"

"I probably will go next Tuesday. I will call them on Monday to confirm it and that is all."

"Sounds good… I start work in my family office next week and I'm excited about my clients. They all have some big problems..."

"So, go to help them…"

"Yes, I will… I miss you already Sophie… I always remember our great times in the library - whether it was reading or studying."

I laugh when I hear Emma. I miss her, of course, but I don't miss my college time. I really want to move forward. I need and want new adventure in my life. But I told her that I miss the old times too.

Emma and I finish our conversation and I pay attention on Conner. He is a very handsome guy and kind of hot and sexy too… Maybe we can hang out tonight. Have a couple glasses of wine, enjoy this beautiful night.

I hear my mom calling my name, little far way:

"Sophie, please, come here."

"Sure mom!" Let's go Conner? They're waiting for us.'

"Of course, Sophie. But before we get there can I ask you to go out today? I will understand if you don't want. I know that you are tired."

"Actually Conner, I want to go out."

"Really? Great! I'll ask your dad if we can have the boat to go out tonight, so we can enjoy this night."

"Sure, go ask for it!"

6 CHAPTER

My mom wanted me to introduce myself to one of our old friends that knew me when I was a young girl. We talked for a while; we laugh remembering old histories that include me in there. But I was just paying attention to what Conner was doing. He talked to my dad, went inside the house, talked to my brother. He also took some wines, cheese and some fruits... he is so kind and gentleman. I probably will kiss him tonight, but nothing more serious. I don't want anything hold me up around here.

Conner called to Maria and asked if the table in the boat was done. We were on our way. Maria answered. I knew it was done, because Conner relaxed a little bit.

It was a beautiful view. The boat was fantastic! There were lights on the tables on the boat. Connor began to unpack what he took at the dinner: fruits, wine and some types of cheese.

Conner put on music while I check the view. I was kind of scared to see the lake at night from the boat, but it's beautiful to see the moon's reflection on the lake's water - a very, very spectacular moment. I stop in the board of the boat and realize I was free of the college and now I will begin my professional life. Conner is coming and bringing a glass of wine... he put on, "Fly Me to the Moon", Frank Sinatra. The music is perfect for the occasion. I am feeling so free and confident about my life...

"Do you remember our first kiss Sophie?"

"Yes, I do Conner..."

"Great time it was..."

I turn around and step down to the table and eat some cheese... I take some green grapes and turn back to Conner. I am a little drunk and can kiss Conner and I will... right now. So, I kissed Conner: it was good. I remember that I did not kissing for a long time...

The music and the wine made everything romantic... the boat stopped in the middle of the lake. I felt kind of scared but to be in the Conner's arms made it worth it. His hands touch my hair so kindly and he kissed my face. I almost fall in love for him. I enjoy this moment. It is so precious for me. I hope Conner don't think it. I'd love to be with him, but I don't love him.

"Sophie, tell me about the college? How

was the experience? Did you learned enough to be a great professional?"

"Well, I loved the experience and yes, I learned enough to be a great professional. I dedicated four years just to the school and I learned a lot... Actually, I am very proud of myself."

Conner made me so comfortable... I can talk to him and tell him my secrets dreams.

"More wine?" He asks.

"Sure, why not?"

From the boat we can see the party at my house. We can even hear people laugh and talk. The lights shine so beautiful in the lake. I can hear also Frank Sinatra from my home's party. My dad loves Sinatra. I love Sinatra too.

Conner start to talk. Conner says that he will go to England for a couple months to get his MBA... also how excited he is.

"That is awesome Conner! Good for you!"

"Come with me Sophie? I think you would love it!"

"I am pretty sure I will, but not now Conner. I will put in practice my knowledge that I get from school!"

"All right pretty girl!"

How blessed I am, to be in this amazing place enjoying my family, feeling free from the college and dream with my future career. I am really blessed.

Conner change the music and put some pop music...we start to dance... and kissing and singing too...

We are having a great time together. I can see the sky...omg the sky is so shine and bright... It is so beautiful...

"Conner, I think I want to go home, I am tired"

"Sure, but it is so early?"

"I guess it is because of the trip from Massachusetts."

"That's fine! Let's go home!"

While Conner drove the boat back to the home, I was paying attention to him. He is so handsome, hot and sexy. Maybe it's because I was a little drunk, but I can see his muscles, his hair and his charm. I can be with him this night.

7 CHAPTER

I wake up the next day around ten o'clock in the morning. My mom wakes me up:

"Good morning darling! Let's go have breakfast!"

"Good morning mom! Can I sleep for a little bit, please?" I groaned.

"Sophie, your dad and your brother need go to work. They are already late. They waiting to you wake up. We want us to have breakfast together."

"That's fine mom. I will be down in a second."

I got up from bed. Brush my teeth put up my hair and went downstairs to have my breakfast with my family.

The table was fantastic: lot fruits, juices and food… Maria is an angel. She always takes care of everything with care and love.

"Good morning sweetheart! How was your night?"

"Good morning dad, good morning brother… It was a great night of sleeping…"

"Good morning Maria. Thank you for breakfast."

"Buenos dias mi amor! Quiere un sucio de naranja?"

"Yes Maria, I want an orange juice, please. So, you guys are late, sorry about it."

"That is fine Sophie, we just want to see you before going to work."

"Any plans today?"

"I don't know Robert. I guess me and mom can go to downtown and have some lunch late."

"It is a great idea Sophie! We can go have some pasta at Terra Ristorante!"

"Sure mom… let's go there!"

My dad and brother went to work. I am not hungry yet.

I just grab a glass of orange juice and sat down at the nook to appreciate the waterfront. This place is very beautiful.

Last night was fun. Me and Conner enjoyed a lot. Maybe we can go out tonight. I took one book in the corner of the table and beginning to ready it. It was a novel "The Last Night We Sleep Together." Very good book. I spent a couple hours reading the book and watching my mom outside of the house help clean up the back yard from the party yesterday. My mom is very organized lady. Always keep the home clean and neat.

She loves a party. So, she is an expert on it. Both, organizing party and the clean up afterwards. I am surprised that Conner did not call me or show up. In other occasions he was here in the early morning. I guess I will go take a shower to go to downtown.

I closed the book, drink my juice and check my mom outside. I go to the kitchen to leave my glass in the sink. I check outside of the windows and I see the flower garden. It is beautiful! I decided to go there and enjoy the flowers. I open the kitchen doors and walk there. The breeze is so pure that I can smell the flowers far away. My dear Lord, those flowers are incredible: colorful and so alive. I will take some red flowers and décor my bedroom. After taking some of those flowers I came back to the kitchen, grabbed a vase, put cold water and put my beautiful flowers. How happy I was to harvest the flowers. I felt peace in my heart.

When I got the stairs to go to my bedroom, my mom appeared,

"Hey Sophie! Let's go to downtown in an hour? Beautiful flowers, did you get them in the garden?"

"Yes mom, I did. Sure, let's go in an hour. I will have a shower and I will be done."

"Great!"

8 CHAPTER

I put my flowers near my bed. It was perfect. I took a shower got dressed, put some makeup and perfume one and left.

My mom was dressed up too. My mom is a beautiful woman. My dad is a luck guy…

"Sophie, I will take the car in the garage and I will be waiting for you on front door, ok?"

"Sure mom!"

I am still thinking why Conner did not contact me yet. It never happens. I meet my mom in the car and we are going to the Terra Ristorante. My mom talking to me about our friends and family till we arrive at the restaurant. I was surprised because she did not say one word about my job in New York. I will talk to her because I want her to go with me on Tuesday.

"Good afternoon Ms. Johnson, your table is available."

"Good afternoon James. Thank you!"

"This is Sophie?"

"Yes, it's me James!"

"Very surprise how she became a beautiful young lady, Mrs. Johnson!"

"Yes, James, she is a very beautiful girl and very smart too!"

"Thank you, guys! Very appreciated!" I said.

When you get back home, everyone talks about you like you're not there and it makes me very uncomfortable. But I can just listen to them and be quiet.

"This place is beautiful; don't you think Sophie?"

"Yes, mom! It is beautiful and cozy."

"The owner of this place is your dad's client. Your dad has a lot of rich clients and it makes our family prosper Sophie. Because of it, your dad and I had a chance to give everything to you and to your brother."

"I know it mom. And I am very grateful. Because of you and dad dedication, I've had a lot of opportunities-"

The waiter came and interrupted my conversation with my mom:

"Good evening Mrs. Johnson! I hope everything is fine."

"Yes, everything is fine, thank you!"

"Something to drink, madam?"

"Sure! Please two glasses of white wine. The best of the house please. I am celebrating my daughter's return from the college."

"This is a great celebration! Welcome home!"

"Thank you!"

So, they talk to little bit and then he leaves. I began to talk to my mom about the opportunities that I have:

"Well, mom, to continue our conversation about opportunities, and how I am grateful to you and dad about everything you guys give to me and to my brother is priceless."

"Thank you darling!"

"Sure, and after I finish my college, with excellent A+ in all my classes, a lot of laws offices invited me to work with them, even one office in China."

"Well done Sophie! Your dad and I are very proud of you. You will be one excellent office owner. Your dad is very excited about you and him to open your own office."

"Mom, I am not will open office with dad! I told dad I want to have some experiences in New York. In this company that I am going Tuesday. And I wish you can go with me."

The waiter come with the wine and water. He serves us and wait for my mom to try the wine and approved it. She shakes her head yes and the waiter leaves.

"Sophie, your dad will be very disappointed as I will. I don't agree with it at all Sophie. All our dedication to you as parents did not compensate."

"Mom, please, don't drive his conversation in a drama. I am an adult woman and I deserve to make my own choices. I want to work in this company in New York."

"This wine is delicious. Did you agree?"

"Yes, mom, it is great..."

Well, I see that I am in trouble with my family. But I have already decided. I will not change my mind.

When I turned around, I see my old friend coming to our table. It's Lia! I did not see her for years and I believe she went to college in California. Maybe she is back home too.

"Hi Sophie! How are you? Oh. My. God. It's been too long! Hey Mrs. Johnson!"

"Hello Lia!" My mom replied.

"Hey Lia!" We hugged each other and talked for a while. She has a table with some friends, and she ended up asking me if I wanted to go to Long Island. One of her friends has a Yacht and they're having a party tomorrow.

"Sure, Lia!"

"I can stop by your house tomorrow and pick you up around ten o'clock. How does that sound?"

Great! I'll be waiting!"

"Excellent, Sophie… Goodbye Ms. Johnson, it was nice seeing you both. I need to go. See you later Sophie."

"See you Lia!"

Lia went back to her table and my mom and I ordered our food. Besides our early conversation about NY, we had a great time together. Some mother and daughter time.

I am thinking too much about Conner… What I am doing? Conner is my ex-boyfriend and we just have a good night together. But I want to spend time with him, before I move to NY. Maybe I will call him later. Maybe he wants to go with me in this party tomorrow.

The lunch come and it looks delicious and fancy! I am okay right now.

We finish our lunch, and I stop by on the Lia's table to say goodbye.

"Bye Lia, I'll see you tomorrow."

"Hi Sophie! Sure, I'll stop by your house tomorrow. Guys this is my high school friend Sophie."

"Hi Sophie!"

Everybody welcomes me. They all look friendly. Of course, I answered hi back to them.

My mom and I was leaving the restaurant and we are going to downtown to shop, buy some bags.

We parked the car and we walked to the stores. My mom and I bought one bag and I decided to buy one bikini, beach hat and sandals. I also bought some sunglasses. For years, I did not spend money on things like this. My money just went to buy books, or extras classes.

My dad called my mom and asked her if she could prepare a nice dinner. One of his clients will come from NY to meeting them. We ended up leaving, she needed time for dinner.

On the way home we stopped to buy some caviar, escargot and oysters for dinner. In the car, she asked me to grab some flowers from the garden. She needed about five bouquets of flowers with different colors. I nodded. She called Maria and ask her to prepare the table for six people. Also, she called the chef to come to our home to organize the dinner.

"Wow, Mom! Well done! You're an expert on preparing dinners."

"My darling…I am a business wife. I am your dad's left and right hand. I help him closed great deals. My dinners are incredible and they welcome people. They show that we are a great family and it demonstrates that they, clients, trust on us."

"When I was younger, I thought you were just stay home mom, just taking care of me and Bob"

"Well Sophie, I did both the business wife and mom. You and brother are the most important things to me and to your dad."

We get home and I just put my shopping bags in my bedroom and I go to pick the flowers. My mom go direct to the dining room talk to Maria.

I just love being here, in the middle of those

flowers. The smell of the flowers and the breeze makes me remember when I was a kid. I can see myself running around this very yard. I ran with our little dog Dinho. He was my best friend. Dinho and me played and get tired so fast. He passed away years ago. I miss him so much. I can see the light of the sunshine from my old days. I laugh to myself, remembering the old times.

"Hey baby!"

I cut some flowers, and look up surprised, it's Conner with a rose.

"Hi Conner!"

"Do you need help with the flowers?"

"Sure, please, you can hold those flowers that I already cut to my mom. I need to cut some more."

"Of course! How was your day today?"

"It was pretty good! I went on a lunch date with my mom and after that we went shopping. Actually, do you remember Lia? The blond girl from high school?"

"Lia, Lia??? I guess I do."

"Yes, she is in the town and was nice to see her. Old times…"

"Great! Do you want to go out tonight,

Sophie? Some friends are going to Long Island, do you want to go?

"Well, I wish I could go. But my dad has an important dinner tonight and I think that is better I'll be here. Also, tomorrow I will go to the sea with Lia. Do want to go? She will be here tomorrow around ten in the morning."

I don't know how, but Conner is so sexy and I am paying too much attention to him. He dresses very well: casual and elegant. He was wearing khaki pants and navy-blue blazer, and he had a perfect haircut, and his cologne was strong. What is going on with me?

"Sorry Sophie, I can't go tomorrow. I already have plans. But maybe we can go out Monday?"

"I don't know about Monday; I have an appointment in NY Tuesday morning."

"Oh, yes. Are you going there by yourself?"

"I hope my mom can go with me, but I am not sure if she wants to go. You know, she doesn't like my idea to move to the City."

"Yes, I heard it about…If you want, I can go with you?"

"Thank you, Conner. I think we are good on the flowers. We have a good amount of the flowers to decorate the table and the living room."

We went to the kitchen and Conner help with the vases. He put water on the vases while I put the flowers on it. After we finished Maria come to the kitchen and said that the vases with flowers came out pretty good. The table will be perfect.

After Conner help me put the vases on the tables and around the living room, he says that he needs to go. I really wanted him to stay for dinner.

I accompanied Conner to the car to say goodbye.

"So, Sophie, let me know if you need me to go to NY, ok?

"Ok Conner, I will. I appreciate it!"

"No problem! See you soon!"

"See you soon Conner!"

He left and I went to my bedroom to choose my dress for dinner.

Just when I got upstairs, I was receiving a phone call. It was Mr. Richard Harris from Partners Group Financial:

"Hello Sophie, it's me Richard Harris from Partners Group Financial in NY. How are you?"

"Hello Mr. Harris! I am fine, thank you."

"So, I am just calling to confirm our

meeting on Tuesday at eleven o'clock at morning."

"Sure, I will be there!"

"That's perfect Sophie! See you on Tuesday at eleven! Thank you!"

"Thank you, Mr. Harris!"

He hung up the phone. I was very excited about this job. It is a dream come true. I took out my resume to just look it over quickly. It could've waited, but I was just so excited.

9 CHAPTER

Around seven o'clock at night, I went to the dinner. Everyone is already there. My father introduced me to his client and we talk for a while. The client's son also went to Harvard. And it gives us an opportunity to talk about the school and teachers.

Later one I grab a glass of wine and I want to see the lake. I step to the porch and appreciate the nature. My parents are so professional, but the dinner brings a little comfort and peace to this new client. Exactly what my parents wanted.

Being here in my home, makes me feel so secure and safe. The thought of moving to NY brings butterflies in my stomach. But I believe it is my time to enjoy my life and my career. The breeze is so refreshing. I appreciate the sky, and the stars at night that look a lot like lights.

"Sophie, please, the dinner is done."

"Thank you, Maria.'

I sit down next to my brother. The chef comes in and introduces the dinner plates. I forgot everything is so sophisticated. When I was in college, we just have our lunch in the dining hall, like, normal.

We ate and it was honestly, perfect. I told my mom that I wanted to go to bed early because tomorrow I will go to the sea. My mom agreed and I said goodbye to my dad, his client and my brother Robert.

I laid down in my bed and I put some music. I don't know, but I cannot get Conner out of my mind. I like to remember him smiling or him trying to help me with my interview in New York. I feel kind of protected around him. He is a kind and gentle spirit. I needed to stop thinking this way. I am moving to NY and Conner will go to Europe for a couple months. I needed to focus on my career.

I woke up the next morning around eight o'clock in the morning. I have a shower, dress up for the boat party. Put sunscreen inside of my bag, extra beach clothes and I am finished and ready to go.

I went downstairs. I went to the kitchen and I made a cup of coffee for myself. Outside was gorgeous. The sunshine was warm and inviting.

At 10:00, literally at 10:00, Lia and her friends

come to pick me up to the party.

To get the yacht we stop at Greenwich Boat and Yacht Club. Lia's friend Brian is the owner his dad owns it.

The yacht was ready, the music was playing and there were drinks. Everyone was very excited. We escort ourselves into the amazing and very chic yacht. We are going to Ocean Beach, Fire Island, in Long Island.

"Hi Sophie, do you like it?"

"Hey Lia, oh yes I love it! Thank you for inviting me to come over. The yacht is fantastic and I need to enjoy a little bit. You know, after finishing college, we are exhausted."

"You're welcome Sophie. Brian is a nice friend and he likes to enjoy new people. There, in the Ocean Beach, we are waiting for more friends come over. There will be more yachts. It is a party with a lot of boats."

"Oh, ok. Nice, it'll be lots of fun."

"For sure Sophie, it will."

It'll be bigger than I thought! That's fine. The view is wonderful. They're playing great music; the blue sky is fascinating and the people here are very happy. My mom texted me asking me where I was... "hahaha ... far away mom... far away," I replied. And I send to her myself pic, making a funny face, I know she'd enjoy. She answered me back:

"OMG, Sophie! Where are you?

"Enjoying my life mom… going to NY for a boat party"

I grabbed a beer, it was a hot day, and I needed to refresh myself. And I see little far away some other yachts stop in the middle of the ocean. There, the music was so loud that we can hear from our boat. People jumped into the water.

We were getting close to the others yachts and our boat was slowing down till we stopped nearby to the other yachts.

People there were dancing, drinking and jumping in the ocean.

When the yacht stop, Brian come to talk to me. He asked me about myself and about my career. He is also a lawyer and has an office in New Canaan, Connecticut. He asked if I am interest to work with him. But I told him no.

"Great move - going to the City. Good choice Sophie!"

"Thanks Brian!"

"Let's go enjoy the party."

"Yes, let's go!"

I laid down in the chairs to get some color. I

needed to tan, as soon as possible. My legs were so white. I grabbed another beer and relaxed in the sun! People were very happy and more and more yachts was approaching with more music, people and happiness.

After a while, when I get tired of the sun, I went to eat something in the inside table. I was so hungry and I needed to go to the bathroom. I look at the mirror and I started to get some color and my hair is long and looks like blonder. I put some lipstick on just to look sexy. I laughed to myself.

I decided to go dance a little bit with the girls and it was a lot of fun. I picked up a beer on my way, because I need it today. Between one song here and there I caught myself thinking and remembering Conner. What's going on with me? Well, he could have come with me. I should insist with him, now, I am enjoying this beautiful day, by myself.

This party is pretty good. Lia called me over and dared me to jump in the ocean with her. I was going to do it.

I stopped at the edge of the yacht, took a deep breath and jumped. I jumped high, I felt the sun and then I went into the cold water. It sent shivers down my spine. The water made my body feel happy and scared all at the same time. I went back to the yacht and people already had towels and drinks for us. It was good.

I start to dry my hair and turned my head to the left and in just a second, looks like I see one face recognized: I can't believe it, do I see Conner? It is Conner! Wait, but he is with another girl and they are kissing. I moved in closer to the edge of the yacht to get a better look. It was him.

10 CHAPTER

Yes, it is Conner! Now I know why he doesn't want to come with me.

"Hey Lia!"

"Yes Sophie!"

"Do you know that guy in that yacht?"

"The blue and white yacht, right?"

"Yes."

"Which guy Sophie? There are so many!" Lia laughed.

"The brunet hair, with white shorts and the blue t-shirt."

"Do you mean Conner?"

"Yes, is he there with the girl?"

"Yes Sophie, it is Conner and Laura."

"Who is Laura?"

"She is Conner's girlfriend. I think they have been dating for a while. She is Brian's cousin. Why? Do you remember him? We graduated from high school together, remember?"

"Yes, I do…"

I left Lia by herself, and I went to the bathroom. I wanted to cry. I looked in the mirror and I felt so foolish. How could Conner kiss me if he had a girlfriend? And why I am upset with him? It was just a kiss on a beautiful night. I cannot understand myself right now. My heart is broken…Really, Sophie? Jealousy? I just want to go home, but it is impossible… I am in the middle of this stupid ocean.

I left the bathroom. I took another beer and I went to tan some more. But, eventually, I got up from the chair and I was going to see Conner again. He was there so happy. He is having so much fun with her. The way he's looking at her he looks like he is in love with her. Then, why did he kiss me?

Well, nothing can change what happened between me and Conner, but see him with his girlfriend hurts me a lot. Just hurt.

After seeing him like a half hour I decided to have a little fun. I jumped again on the water, I danced and drank more. I was doing everything by myself...and that's fine. I guess...

I convinced my mom to come with me to New York in my interview.

My dad helped me out and told my mom to come to NY with me. She was resilient, but at the end we convinced her to come with me.

We get at NY around 9:00 am. We stop at a parking and we go to enjoy little bit NY.

"Sophie, NY is very beautiful but it is a very busy city. I could never live here - very busy city!!!"

"In college and it was very calm and relaxed. Now I need to enjoy different fillings. I like it already..."

We walked to Times Square... We stopped at Starbucks for a coffee.

Around 10:15am we walk to the building that I will be interviewed. It was located at 1114 6th Avenue with 42nd Street in the W.R. Grace Building.

We get in the front of the building. The view is so beautiful: it overlooks Bryant Park and the New York Library.

"Sophie. I'm going to head to the library while you will go to the interview.

"Sure, I appreciate your patience to come

over with me, mom. I hope you enjoy it!"

"Of course, I will. Good luck in the interview my daughter!"

"Thank you, mom!"

"No problem baby!

My mom went to the library while I make my way to the building.

So, I took a deep breath, brushed off my clothes and called the elevator.

When the elevator doors open, I see a lot of movement. My legs are shaking and I walk in the direction of the receptionist.

"Good Morning. I am Sophie Johnson and I have an interview appointment with Mr. Richard Harris at eleven."

"Good morning Ms. Johnson! He is waiting for you in the room, seven. You can go straight in this way and they left. The room number seven will be in your right."

"Ok, Thank you very much!"

"No problem!"

I am not late. It is 10:45am and he is already waiting for me. I am so nervous. It will be my first job and it makes nervous.

When I got to the room and I knocked on the door and I hear a voice saying:

"Please, come in!"

I open the door slowly as I can. My legs keep shaking and when I saw Mr. Richard Harris, I felt more nervous. He is sitting in a meeting table reading my resume. He got up from his chair and came in my direction. We shake hands and I sat next to his chair.

He is a handsome man. Mr. Richard Harris is around his thirties. Dress very well and looks very professional. I am nervous and I think he can fell it.

"Good morning Ms. Sophie!"

"Good morning Mr. Harris!"

"I am very impressed with your resume Ms. Johnson. Well done in the college and we are very excited about you!"

"Thank you, Mr. Harris! Thank you very much for accepting my resume and I am very happy to be here."

We changed conversations. He asked me about my dad's lawyer career, about my future idea and much more. I felt very comfortable talking to him. He is very young man and handsome one. He smile is very sexy and sometimes I'd get lost in his smile. We talked for like an hour and after the interview he asked me if I want to work with the company. The salary is very interesting. The benefits are great and for me, the experience will be amazing and that's the most important

We shake hands again and I left the office room. Once I accepted the job, I need go the Human Resources department to fill up all the paperwork. I wanted to scream so badly. I am very happy and it was so easy to be hired... I am kind of proud of myself. It was worth all the sacrifice dedicated to the studies. Now I will make money and will begin building my career.

I stopped at the human resources department and I filled out all the paperwork and, I will start to work next Monday.

I needed to find an apartment! Maybe my mom can help me out today. It slipped my mind!

I left the building smiling. I stop in the front at the Grace Building and I imagined myself every day coming to work. The cars, the yellow taxis and a lot of people walking through the busy streets making me feel at home. Yes, NY will be my home from now on.

I walk into the library to meet my mom and am thinking about how to give her the news. I will not be surprised if she will be sad with the news, but she needs to understand me and understand my decision.

When I got the library, I saw her in the back of it and she was reading a book.

"Hey mom!"

"Hey darling! How it was? I am very excited to know the news?"

"Well mom, now I need to move to NY until next Monday!!!"

"Oh my god, Sophie! Congratulations my daughter. I am very happy for you!"

"Really mom? I thought you will be sad…"

"Of course not, Sophie. I wish you can work with your dad, but that's fine! If you are happy of course, we will be happy!"

"Thank you, mom, for your support. It means a lot to me. I'm in shock! I need to find an apartment and everything…"

"Sophie don't worry. My friend Rose is an owner of a realtor company and we will contact her and ask her to find an apartment for you."

"Awesome mom! That's such a good idea. Thank you."

We hugged each other and we decided to walk down 5th Avenue and have a late lunch. My mom was excited about my new job and for myself to be all moved to NY. She also agreed with me to find an apartment near my job. We will probably pay more, but at least I don't need a car. The NY traffic is crazy.

11 CHAPTER

I've never felt so happy. I even remember Conner, he almost broke my heart, but I am alive. And I will never see him again...I hope!

In my mind right now is just thinking about the future. My new home, my career and new friends.

After we walked a lot, shopping in some stores we decide to stop to lunch and celebrate my new job.

We love this restaurant Sushi Ginza Onodera; they prepare amazing plates and my mom and I want to eat sushi today.

We got there around 1:30pm and we were hungry. We were walking for so long and my feet were hurting. We haven't been there in so long and it's so good.

We find a table very cozy and we ask for a water. My mom looks so happy that I can't believe it.

"I will ask for a bottle of champagne to celebrate your new job Sophie! I am very happy and proud of you!"

"I am happy too mom. When Mr. Richard ask me if I want to work with him, I couldn't believe it."

The waiter came over and ask if we need a drink and my mom ask for a champagne.

Between the water and champagne my dad call and ask my mom how my interview and my mom had told him the news. Looks like between their conversation, that my dad is happy too.

I felt so relieved to know that my parents are accepting and celebrate my decision and my success. I was scared and kind of frustrated, but now everything is working well.

The chef Saito came over to our table and explain the menu to today's lunch.

We decide following his suggestion: Omakase Course - A 15 pieces of Nigiri, Miso and Desert, by Chef Saito.

My mom and I were a little drunk and we laughed about everything around us. We were happy and I am so glad to have her by my side in this victory. I am so proud of myself. We were having so much fun in the City. I told my mom that she always can come over and stay with me for a couple days, when I am established in my apartment.

After Lunch, I called our drive, Javier, to pick us up at the restaurant. We are a little drunk and we have some bags from the shopping that we did earlier today.

Javier stopped by the restaurant and we drive back home.

When we drive back home, I really enjoy the view. From the road I can see the Hudson River, people running or on their bikes. New York it is a lovely city.

I took my cell phone and I texted to Conner:

"I LOVE NY!"

He texted me back immediately…

"Hey stranger! How was your interview?"

"Well, I have a great job and I will start to work on Monday…"

"Wow, congratulations!!! Looks like it was very easy?"

"Yes, I guess…"

"Can we have a dinner together to celebrate?"

"No I'm sorry, I am tired and I need my bed… Today

was a very busy day and I need to relax."

"Maybe tomorrow? And why didn't you answer my messages since Sunday? Is there something wrong?"

When Conner asked me this question, I want to answer him that I was mad at him, because he was kissing another girl... in the boat... and I guess I was jealous about this...

"Nothing Conner, I didn't answer you because I was busy.

I will never tell Conner that I saw him with that girl -- his girlfriend. I just don't understand why he is calling me while he is in love with her. I just don't understand.

"Can I call you tomorrow?"

"No, Conner. I need to find an apartment. Maybe we can see each other in another time. Ok? I just wanted to share with you that I have a job in NY."

"Ok, that's fine. If you need anything let me know."

"Sure, I will."

We get home and I was very tired, but very satisfied. My dad had a bouquet of a beautiful flower. He gave it to me as a congratulations. I was so tired that I hug him and I went to my bedroom.

I had a shower and I went straight to my bed.

I heard my mom outside my bedroom saying:

"Sophie, tomorrow we need to go to find your apartment, ok?"

"Sure, mom, sure…" I replied.

12 CHAPTER

I wake up next morning around eleven o'clock. It is late for someone that needs to find an apartment quickly in NY. But I was exhausted and I needed a good night of sleep. I went downstairs and called Maria to the kitchen and she gave me a great breakfast… it was amazing. Maria started to talk to me about how I will need to learn how to cook, because now I will live by myself and to eat every day in a restaurant is not as healthy.

"I know Maria. I promise that I will learn how to cook…"

"Ok Sophie, I will go there one day to try your food…"

"Sure, Maria, you will love my food!"

"I hope so!"

I had a blessed breakfast. It gave me a lot of energy. I ask to Maria where was my mom and she said that my mom left early today.

I took a shower and I decided to visit my dad in his office.

Before I left the house, my mom texted me and asked me if I could meet her in her friend's realtor office. Of course, I agreed and I drove to the office. When I get there mom already was there and they were looking for some renting options near my job in NY.

"Hello Sophie, my darling. This is Ana. She is the owner of this realtor office and we found some great options for you."

"Nice to meet you Mrs. Ana. Thank you for helping me out. I was stressed out when I found out that I needed a place as fast as Monday."

"Nice to meet you too Sophie. It is my pleasure to help you and your mom to figure it out this situation. We found three great options. All of them are nearby to your new office."

"Excellent! I am very excited to see all of them."

Mrs. Ana showed me all the three options. I liked a three of them. One is on 48th Street, another at 28th Street and another at 31st Street. We looked at the pictures of the apartments. My mom asked Mrs. Ana if it would be possible to see them. She said it is possible. She just needs to call and make an appointment or borrow the keys to each place.

We exchange some information and the documentation that is needed to rent one of those places.

"Mom, I am kind of stressed about finding a place for me."

"No need to worry about it Sophie. Everything will be alright. Ana will find a great place for you. Trust me."

"I know, I know. I was thinking we could go to dad office and get a lunch around there."

"Great idea Sophie, I will ask him if he is available."

I am happy and excited about my new job. Lia sent a text to me asking if I wanted to go out tonight. I texted back yes.

"Sophie, your dad is waiting for us."

"Nice mom. I miss his office too. Is the Martha still his secretary?"

"Yes, she is. A great helper for your dad to have…"

Mrs. Martha worked with my dad for decades and she is a great employee. My dad trusts her very much, she is very professional. My mom said that Mrs. Ana already had two of those apartments available to us to check on them tomorrow. I jumped and hugged my mom which was a surprise to her.

"Sophie, be more careful!"

"Mom, this is my life and I am happy that things are going well…"

We walked to the cars and we drive to my dad's office.

He was there with a big smile waiting for me and my mom. We hugged each other and he invited me to see the new offices and the new big meeting room. He is a very hard worker and very smart too.

"Sophie, my dream is for you to work with me. The place I had in mind to us be a partner was next to this building. It is a big place with numerous offices. We will probably make tons of money."

"Dad, I'd really love to work with you, but for right now…"

"I know, I know and I wish the best for you there my daughter. The place that you will work is a fantastic place to begin your career. I am very proud of you that you got a job there."

"Thank you, dad. It means a lot. I really appreciate it."

"Let's go have lunch? Nearby here we have a great place: we have Italian, Mexican or steak house restaurant? You guys pick one."

Any one was okay with me, I just wanted a salad and so, I went with the flow.

We had a blessed lunch. I talked to my dad and shared my plans and he agreed with everything. I am guessing that he is just wanting to make me happy. My mom just smiled here and there, but she was quiet just enjoying my dad and I's conversation.

13 CHAPTER

Around nine at night I dressed up to meet Lia and her friends at the bar. My mom offered a ride, but I told her I wasn't drinking. I Just wanted to talk to some friends.

I get the bar and Lia already was there. The bar was crowded. I saw Lia's table and I walked through and got there. I said hello to everyone and I grabbed a glass of water. The music was loud and people were having fun.

I was looking around and pray to not see Corner here. My head turned in each part at this bar and no sign of this guy. God, thank You!

We talk with each other. Lot kids just come from the college and all of them are happy: ones because found a job, others because come back home and others are just happy or drunk.

My mom texted me saying she plans to leave early tomorrow. We have three apartments to check on. I texted her back asking what time she wanted to leave. She answered back: "I don't know Sophie. I am just going with you to see your home. So, tell me, what time we need to leave to the City?" I told my mom that we will leave around seven in the morning. She agreed. I got up and went to the bar to get a drink before I left.

"Hey, can I have a Cosmopolitan please?" I asked.

"Sure!"

While I was waiting for a drink this handsome guy come close to me and we started to talk. My dirty Martini came, but I did not go back to the table that I was at. This guy and I had some fun conversation and he has the sexiest smile I could see. We talked and laughed, he touched my shoulder occasionally, and would come very close to my face to tell me anything. If I was a little drunk, I can kiss this handsome boy.

Between our conversation I just see Conner and Laura come in the bar. My heart began beating so fast, that I can't believe it. Why I am feeling that way? Was I the rebound girl? I don't know what it means, but I just didn't want to see them together.

My Cosmopolitan is gone and I decide to leave. The guy asked me if he did something wrong, because I was leaving so early. I just said that I needed to be in NY tomorrow morning. So, I needed to leave. I stopped at Lia's table to say goodbye to everyone and they answered goodbye back.

When I step out of the bar, I felt someone grab my arm:

"Hey stranger" It was Conner.

"Conner!" I slapped his chest "You scared me to death!"

"Sorry sorry, I didn't know you were here!"

"Well you don't know nothing about me Conner!"

He tilted his head in confusion "Are you mad at me or something? I called you all week and you never call or text me back."

"Sorry Conner, I am very busy because I need to organize things to move to New York."

"Well, being at the bar doesn't look busy."

"Conner, I need to leave. I need to go to NY tomorrow early in the morning. So, I need to go!"

"That's fine Sophie! If you need anything let

me know I guess…"

I get in the car wishing I could just scream at Conner and spill everything on that I knew about him and his girlfriend. Gosh, is this guy stupid or what? I just turned the radio on and the song playing was Selena Gomez's "Back to you.":

"And every time we talk

Every single word builds up to this moment

And I got to convince myself I don't want it

Even though I do

You can break my heart in two…"

I wanted to cry so much and I felt this little pain. He was my ex-boyfriend and he was part of my old life, the one I left back in Boston. I wanted nothing to do with him.

14 CHAPTER

We left my home to New York around seven. I was tired and I need a cup of coffee.

I asked for our driver, Javier, to stop by at Starbucks to buy a coffee and my mom yelled at me saying why I did not drink coffee at home.

"Mom, I need Starbucks Coffee… it is so delicious!"

"Ugh. Ok…"

We stopped to buy my coffee and we drive to NY. The Merritt Parkway was not that bad and we got in NY, Manhattan in forty minutes.

We meet Mrs. Ana at the first apartment that was located on the 235W 48th. At first, I love the entrance. The lodge was very nice and I like the decoration. I can see myself going and coming from my job. The distance walking is like twelve minutes. I agree it is good, almost perfect for the people living and working in the City.

The apartment was a good size with two bedrooms, one and a half bathrooms, living room, small dining room and a kitchen. For me it was perfect.

"Mom, I think I like this place. I don't need to see another apartment."

"No Sophie. You should look at others too. Maybe the other one is better than this one."

"Mom, please, I want this one. I love the decoration and fit perfect to my needs."

"I don't know Sophie… What do you think Ana?"

"Well, I think she should see the others, but at least this one is closest to her job. So, she can go walking with no problem at all."

"See, mom. This apartment it is amazing."

"Well, if you like it and everything looks fine let's lease it Ana."

"Sure, Leila. I will contact the owner and later today or tomorrow Sophie can sign the lease contract."

"Awesome… see mom! I am easy girl."

"Yes, Sophie… You are…"

We left the building and we decided to go back home. We will stop in some store in Greenwich to buy some home things for my new home like towels, bath and bedroom mats, and some personal décor.

When I looked at my cellphone, I saw that I had some emails and one was from my company. I open the email and it was a meeting schedule for next Monday at eleven o'clock in the morning in room nine to discuss a client tax evasion problem. And the documentation is on file. I open the file and it has around forty-five pages.

What??? OMG, I need to read this and process it for Monday, bring some solutions and move to New York.

I never shopped so fast in entire of my life… I didn't even have inspiration to buy some décor for my new place.

I just needed to go back home and beginning to ready this process. My mom told me to relax, but it will not change my feeling to leave for home as soon as we can.

"Mom, please, let's go!"

"Calm down Sophie… at least we need to pay for those things…"

When I got home, I ran to my room. I opened my email and click to open to the file sent by the company. This was a case from a client in California and his case was about tax evasion. The IRS is auditing the client company and they are asking for many unnecessary documentations. So, I spent all my evening and night studying the case. I went to my dad's library and took some books about tax and regulation of IRS.

Maria brought me soup and salad. I was exhausted. I needed a break. My mom came to my room and I said to her that I need to study the client case. So, I need to be prepared to move to NY and study the case. But tomorrow we need box a lot of the clothes and things for the new home. At least the apartment is furnished.

I turned the lights off and went to sleep.

15 CHAPTER

My first day in the office. I am excited but nervous. I went to work around 7:00 am. I am supposed to work every day at 10:00am till 3:00pm. But I want to see my office and organize for the meeting. I dress up very professional in a business suit. I think for the first day it is appropriate.

I know my office it is the number eight. I got there, put some offices supplies, books and my suitcase.

I went to see people around but not many people were around. I ask the receptionist where was the coffee machine and she explains where the kitchen was. When I got in the kitchen, I was very surprised how big and beautiful it was. I took a cup and I make coffee. While I was waiting for my coffee Mr. Richard came into the kitchen. I got so nervous; I don't know why but I felt uncomfortable with him around. He is a very handsome man. Looks so strong and smart.

"Good morning Sophie! Nice to see you early! Welcome aboard"

"Good morning Mr. Richard Harris!"

"Please, Sophie, never call me Mr. Richard… everyone around calls me Rich and I appreciate if you call me the same."

"Sure Rich!" It was weird.

"So, today at eleven o'clock in the morning, we have a meeting. Did you receive the material?"

"Yes, I did and I had an opportunity to read and find solutions for this case."

"Well done, Sophie. Let's discuss it later. Did you find your office? Did you like it?"

"Yes, I found my office and I love it. Thank you for asking."

"See you later Sophie."

"See you later Rich."

I took my cup of coffee and I went to my office. While I was walking to my office, I meet this attorney Eva. She was cordial with me and welcomed me to the group. I try to be nice and rush to my office to check the last details about the case for the meeting. When I got to my office, I see a pallet of file in my desk. Gosh what is this?!

In my desk have four more other cases… Well, lot job around here, Jesus Christ!

I got home around 8:00 pm and I am exhausted. Today was a very busy day. In the meeting for the tax case I had a great presentation and they gave me the case. I already filed it.

I open a bottle of wine and I called for deliver food: pasta and salad… they will deliver the dinner in one hour and a half. I am so hungry. I miss Maria so much right now. I brought one case to study it in my home. About tax issue again. People need to start paying taxes man…

The wine it is perfect and I really enjoy my place. I took my glass of wine and start walking in my new apartment… The living room is fancy and cozy. How beautiful is see the busy City from my windows…Lights and people make downstairs. Splendid! I love New York City. I love living in Manhattan, it is magical.

Back to the case. I sit down on the floor in the living room and start to pass the pages…one by one… it will be an easy case. Took couple books to check it…

The phone rang and it was my delivery guy going upstairs with my dinner. This guy is my savior for tonight.

After dinner I just need my bed... I needed a good night of sleep...

16 CHAPTER

Got to the office early again... work, work and work...

After a week I felt very happy with my job. It is a lot of work and I did my work on time...I received a lot of compliments and both of my bosses congratulated me for a great first week.

It was Friday and I was already to leave. Rich came to my office and invited me to go to one office party in the Yacht's owner. I didn't know how to answer. I was very tired and I wanted to go home. But, to not accept the invitation it is kind of rude.

"Sure, I want to go Rich. But how I can get there?"

While he's talking to me, his phone rings, and

he answers his phone. I organize my desk in the meantime. I will bring home one more case to read for a meeting on Monday. He pauses his conversation on the phone, and says:

"Sophie, you can go with me with if you'd like" as he shoots a smile

In the same time Eva pass by my office and offer a ride to me for the party and I accepted. Rich just shakes his head yes and left the office.

Eva and I just exchanged a couple words and we drive to the party.

We got there. Almost everyone was there. The yacht was the most beautiful yacht that I have ever seen in my life. It was very fancy and very chic. There's a lot of food, drinks and waiters serving all employees of the office. A very interesting collection of music. Mostly Frank Sinatra and some pop music.

When I try to talk to Eva she already left and went to talk to other girls from office. I get the feeling that people around the office try to avoid my presence. It is hard, but I really don't care that much. My focus is my job right now and really, I don't need friends, especially those one.

I took one glass of wine and I went to appreciate the moon. It was fantastic. The reflection of the moon on the Hudson river was impeccable.

Nor can I describe the charm of that. While the yacht departed to the river Frank Sinatra was playing. This is what I need right now to relax and enjoy the beauty of nature. From here I can see the lights of Manhattan. It is beautiful.

I leaned against the edge of the yacht and slowly I turned to the party. People are having a lot of fun: they are dancing, drinking and smiling but I just wanted to feel the breeze in my hair and my face, it was good. I close my eyes for a while and Conner came to my memories. I miss him and everybody from Greenwich, even my friends from college: Emma and Jerry. Some fun memories with them, great old times.

"Are you are having some fun?"

"Hey Rich! Yes, I am… This moment it is great and relaxing for me. Thank you for inviting me."

"You don't like to dance?"

"Yes, I do, but now and just want to be quiet for a while…"

"Another glass of wine?" Rich asked me.

"Definitely."

Rich went to take a glass of wine. He is so charming and probably his girlfriend is here or some other place else.

He came back with my glass of wine and we started to talk. While we were talking, I saw one group of girls look at us and I figure they made some comments, probably about Rich and me.

"Sophie, do you like living in the City?"

I took my glass of wine and I look back to the wonderful view: reflection of the moon in the river. It was so relaxing. Rich kept talking to me.

"I can't live in the City... It is too busy and when I get home, I need a good place to relax..."

He leaned against the edge of the yacht very close to me, so I turned my face to continue the conversation and move away from him. When I turned my face to him, my eyes met his eyes and I just lost myself: his eyes was so fixed on me and on my eyes that seemed to control me. He has a beautiful blue eyes, my whole body, my breath and even the beating of my heart stopped there, in that moment it seemed I was hypnotized by him. He smiled at me while I turned my face to our conversation and he continue talking.

"Sophie, do you like to work in the company?"

Well, I was confused for a little bit, this handsome man standing by my side and his charming can control my thinking. So, I started to talk and tried not to look like a young girl that doesn't know how to handle a guy.

"So, Richard Harris, for the first question my answer is yes. I am loving the City… I think NY had a beautiful charming energy even being a big city!"

I took a sip of wine, turned my face around the party to not be so fixed into Rich eyes…

"Yes, I love working here. People are very professional, not that friendly, but professional."

"Everyone in the office just worry about themselves, Sophie. Nobody cares…"

"I know that, but I am too busy to worry about people at work. I am not that self-centered, but we are people looking to prosper. We don't need people around us trying to be nice with us."

We talked and laughed, while people danced. There was a DJ, his music choice was questionable for the most part.

Eva came to us and call us to go dance with others. I nodded my head yes and walked to the group of people that was dancing. Rich did not come with us. He was standing by the edge of the yacht. Sometimes I caught him looking at me. I didn't know if he was flirting with me or he just wanted to be nice to me. Maybe it was because I was new in the office or I don't know...

I had my fourth glass of wine and I was a little drunk. I was thinking to myself what time those people going home. I went downstairs to go to the bathroom and I saw Rich on his cell phone. It looks like he was fighting, maybe with his girlfriend.

When I left the bathroom, I bumped into Rich, literally. He is a tall guy and my face hit his chest.   He smelled so good. Dear Lord, help me...

"I am sorry Rich!"

He held my arms with his strong hands and set me aside and did not say one word and left.

I followed him outside, but I did not have a chance to ask him if he was ok, instead I went to Eva and ask her what time the party will be done and she said in about an hour or so.

I stood there in the corner looking to the river again, but this time, by myself. Rich was talking with some guy and never looks back to me.

Eleven thirty we got back to the marine and Eva give me a ride to my home.

17 CHAPTER

Next Monday, in the office, another meeting other cases... more and more cases.

I enjoy my new job, my office but I miss my home. It's not good to be alone every day and in the office. I did not have a chance to make any friends. After the work some girls go out to bars, but they never invite me. Some guys do the same. They go out and spend a couple hours together and done. I took my files of cases to study home. I open a bottle of wine and enjoy the night. Order food and done. Weeks and weeks of that. Besides the yacht party, I did not hang out with the people of the office.

Every night my mom texted me asking me if I

am ok and I texted back: "I am great mom! :)"

Another day, Conner texted me asking about my new job and office. I decided not to answer him.

Life keeps going on…

It is Friday and I can't believe I was free. This weekend I will take a train and go see my parents in Greenwich. I miss them. I've been here alone every day; I am just home sick. When I was leaving the office, Rich call me in his office. There was Rich and Angelo, the NY supervisor:

"Angelo, this is Sophie the young girl that I was talking about. She is in on numerous cases and almost all of them were filled by her and we are having great progress in the tax department."

"Hello Mr. Angelo!"

"Hello Sophie. I am hearing about your job and the owner, Mr. Philip, asked me to come here to meet with you! We are very happy with you, this job, and the company and we need you to fly to California with Mr. Richard for a meeting tomorrow."

"I don't think it is a problem, right Sophie?" Richard asked me.

"Of course not."

"Sorry for such a late notice, but the jet will

be departing at 7:00pm."

"That's fine Mr. Angelo. I will be here at 5:30pm".

"Great Sophie, really appreciate it."

"Nice to meet you Mr. Angelo."

What? California? I texted my mom and canceled my visit there in her home.

I went to Eva's office and asked her about this type of meeting in California and she said:

"What are you saying to me Sophie? Did Mr. Angelo ask you to go to California?"

"Yes, and I don't know if I need to take a lot of clothes or what?"

"Bastards! Go naked Sophie, I don't care! Sophie, just get out of my office... I am super busy."

"Oh, okay, Eva... Sorry..."

She turned her chair back to me and I left her office. So, I guess she was waiting for this opportunity and I stole it from her.

I run to my apt and took clothes, put them in my small bag, add makeup, deodorant, toothbrush and a small bottle of perfume. Never did I ever pack a bag so fast. I was out the door.

While I was waiting for them, I organized my file for Monday. Sent a couple of emails and studied the last case I have with me.

Rich stop by my office and said.

"Sophie, please, bring your last presentation with you. It will be an example in the meeting for the tax case."

"Sure, of course Rich Harris!"

I copied the presentation in the flash drive and done!

18 CHAPTER

Rich and I took a car from the company and the driver left us in the JFK Airport. The jet was there waiting for us. Also, there were a lot of people from the office. It was around six people...

Rich didn't even exchange a word with me. He was very concentrated on his computer. Everyone was. So, I put my last presentation on my laptop and I start to check on it.

Rich turned his face on me and said:

"Sophie, tomorrow you will be the first one to talk in the meeting, ok? Prepare you data show presentation for it"

I sat down next to Rich and asked what would

be going on in this meeting, because I was kind of lost…

"Oh yeah Sophie! You are new here. I will explain: Every six months the company holds a meeting to guide everyone to following the best winners' cases. Yours were one of those. So, people will try to use your arguments to win cases. So, do, please, your best tomorrow."

"Ok, I will."

I sat back in my seat and paid more attention to my work and tried to see myself in this meeting room tomorrow.

It was a lot of pressure, but let's go.

We got to Los Angeles very late and everyone went to the Hotel. Taxis and limos was waiting for us. No one exchanged words and when we arrive into hotel everyone took the room's keys and run to get some sleep.

My alarm went off around six thirty in the morning. I was so tired but I needed to wake up. I took a great shower and dressed up for the meeting. Makeup on and very professional hair. I looked like a very professional young woman and was about to have a great meeting. I went downstairs around eight thirty to have breakfast.

The elevator doors opened and I got in. In two

seconds, I saw a hand hold the elevator doors. It was Rich. He had a New York Times newspaper in his hands and didn't look at me. He continued reading the newspaper and I looked at my hair in the elevator's reflection.

When the elevator opened on the lobby floor, it was when Rich noticed and said:

"Good morning Sophie! I am sorry, I was focused on my newspaper. Are prepared for the meeting today?"

"Good morning Rich! Yes, I am."

"We will leave the hotel to go to the meeting at ten o'clock. The driver will be outside of the hotel, ok?"

"No, problem…I'll be around."

I took one table and put my suitcase and my laptop in one chair. I went to the breakfast table to grab some fruits and some bread. The waiter brought me orange juice and a cup of coffee. In about a half hour everyone started to show up to have a breakfast. Their faces were tired and exhausted. I just hoped that my makeup was covering my tired face.

Around nine thirty, the limos started to park in front of the hotel. Rich called everyone to get in the ride. It was very exciting and nice new job, with responsibilities and I am very happy to be the one to talk about my job and my experiences as an attorney in this meeting.

Two thirty in the afternoon in the same day, we all prepared to go back to NY. In six hours, I would probably be in my own home.

I was reading a book about tax law from California when Rich seat down next to me and said:

"Great job today Sophie! I am impressed with your professionalism and dedication. Keep it alive in your heart and all your dreams will come true."

"Thank you, Rich Harris! It means a lot to me."

He got up from the seat next to me and seat down in his own seat. My legs were shaking with Rich words. My chest will explode with so much emotion. I didn't even know that I was that good. I needed to relax and I asked for a glass of whiskey.

19 CHAPTER

After this I slept pretty good during the flight back to NY.

I woke up around one o'clock in the afternoon on Sunday. My mom said she wants me to go to have lunch with them.

"Please Sophie! Come over. Everyone will be here. I can send the driver to pick you up and drive you back."

I am so tired because the flights going to and from California. But I miss my mom and dad. So, I decide to go see them in Greenwich.

I left my shower and I saw that my phone have a message. I look at the message and it was

Rich…what does he want on a Sunday afternoon?

"Hi Sophie, sorry bothering you this afternoon, but we're having a small party in the yacht around six o'clock…do you want to go? I can pass by for you. Rich."

Wow… now I don't know what to do. Actually, I know. I want to go to Rich party…

"Hello Rich, that's fine. You are not bother me at all. Sure, I want to go."

"Can I pass by for you around four o'clock?"

"Yes, that's a good time."

"So, see you at four Sophie!"

"Thank you, Rich."

I don't know why, but when Rich talks to me I feel butterflies in my stomach. I'm excited.

I don't know anything about Rich, but it is just a business party. He is very handsome and it is very hard for me to keep the idea that he is my boss. The way he looks at me, it is just professional eye contact. But, when he gets close to me, my legs, my hands, my everything shakes.

I dressed up very casual for every yacht party, but I want to look hot and sexy too, no I can't, I can't dress up sexy or hot.

You know what? I will open one bottle of wine

and put some music on and I will relax a little bit. Gosh, I am very nervous. I put U2 and enjoy my glass of wine.

I danced a little bit and looked in my closet to decide which clothes I will go to this party... black dress.

At four o'clock Rich texted me saying that he was downstairs waiting for me. I rushed myself here and there and I run to keep Rich from waiting.

"Hi Rich! Thank you for the invitation for the party and for the ride."

"No problem, Sophie!"

Oh my god, he smells so good! My head blow out with this cologne. And as always, Rich looks very handsome. God help me to be a good girl.

We talked about the meeting in California. He told me that the owners are happy with my job. I thanked him.

We took around one hour to get to the yacht. During the drive to the party we talked a lot and Rich was very charming and funny. Looks like the party was more relaxed and casual then to do business. Rich was very relaxed and happy. I never seen him like that.

When we got inside of the yacht, I noticed that there were not a lot of people there. No one from our office, actually, just us and Bryan, from the financial department.

"Sophie, this party is just for a couple people. The owners will be here later and not many employees are inviting. They ask to meet you tonight."

"Oh wow, Rich. Should I do something or tell them something?"

"No, no Sophie. Just be yourself. This party is for new good lawyers, like yourself."

"Oh ok. I got this...

Rich was by my side the entire party. He brought me a glass of wine. We kept talking for a few hours. I feel so comfortable talking to Rich. We have a great connection. When we look to each other, or when we talk or even when we exchange ideas feels like we understand each other very well.

The weather was excellent, and the Hudson River was so calm, that made your trip so calm.

The music playing was perfect: jazz. I am not a fan of jazz, but it was so perfect that I couldn't complain. I don't know if I like jazz now or maybe Rich made me like it.

The DJ changed the music and put some Caribbean music on. Rich asked me to dance. I laughed because I can't dance Caribbean music at all. He pushed me to dance with him in the center of the floor. Other couples danced there, so I started to dance with Rich.

We danced to a couple of Caribbean songs and we had a lot of fun. He dances well. I was surprised to see how fun of a guy Rich is. In the office he looks like a pain in our ass boss, and he is.

We stop for a little while to drink a glass of wine. I wanted to ask him if he has a girlfriend, but he is my boss and if I ask him this, it doesn't look very professional. But today I feel that Rich is very close to me. The way he talks and look into my eyes, today is different. He looks free, free to me, free for me, and I enjoy it.

"So, Sophie... How old are you?"

"Rich, this is not a good question to ask a lady..."

"Let me guess: twenty-four?"

"Yes, it is..."

"Do you have a boyfriend?"

When he asked me this question, I felt so in love with him. My guess was that he wants to know if I am available. Available for a relationship? Maybe I am?

The lights come from the sky... it was the

helicopter.

"They are here…"

Rich said. The owners had arrived. It was around seven thirty at night.

20 CHAPTER

The helicopter landed on top of the yacht, in the helipad.

Everyone was meeting inside of the yacht waiting for the owners. Rich was greeting them and brought them up to the dining area.

They were two brothers. They look around their forties or fifties. They came right up to me, both of them:

"Hello Sophie! Thank you very much for coming tonight. We really appreciate it."

"It is my pleasure Mr. Philip and Mr. Paul."

"Is Richard taking care of you?" ask Mr. Paul.

"Yes, he is…"

"How was the trip?" Rich asked them.

"It was good, man. Thank you for the party Rich. All those employees are from NY?" Mr. Philip ask while Mr. Paul took a glass of wine from the tray. Both brothers looked around and offered a smile for everyone in the party.

"Most of them. Two are from Connecticut, the new office."

"Great! Let's go party. Thank you again Sophie for coming and great job in the office."

"Thank you very much Mr. Philip."

"Sophie, excuse me for a second I need to introduce them to the new employees, ok?"

"That's fine Rich, no problem."

While Rich went around with the bosses, I went outside to get some fresh air.

Tonight, was intense for me. They came in my direction and I was the first person that they wanted to meet. I am very proud of myself. I know I am very good at my job, but I am excellent! I took my fourth or fifth glass of wine tonight. I leaned against the edge of the yacht and stared at that beautiful moon and its brightness cheered my soul. I am feeling very happy to be here and enjoying my success, it's so good. I smile to myself and remembering the same moon that I saw when I left the library on late night after a long study hall in the college.

In a half hour I heard someone come in my direction, it was Rich. He came with a big smile on his face. I smile back to him. I didn't know what was going on but Rich was very happy.

"Let's go dance again Sophie?"

"Sure, let's go."

He grabbed me by the waist and woke me up to dance. I think he did not even notice, but he kissed my neck.

We danced a lot and we looked like a nice couple. Or at least people told us that while we were dancing. I am so happy dancing with Rich. Being so close with him, makes my heart beat fast… I am crushing on Rich.

We stopped dancing and went for some fresh air. But before we took some wine.

"Sophie, you are a very smart girl and you are very fun. I love working with you and we have great times as well.

"I love being around you Rich."

We were a little drunk. We were laughing so much and we did not pay attention to others around us. I just remember when I saw Bryan talk to Rich asking if he was ok and if he needed a ride home. Rich told him that he was fine.

21 CHAPTER

The owners left in the helicopter after two hours of enjoying the party on the yacht. Rich and I was on the helipad to say goodbye to them. When the lights of the helicopter disappeared, everyone went back to their business.

I know we are drunk and the music helped this happen, but I feel Rich's hands hold my head and push me up to his lips. We kissed. I kissed him with so much love and confused feelings. I just enjoyed it so much.

We kiss so long. Looks like Rich and I did not kiss someone for a long time and we needed this time to us... for us.

The mixture of the music, drinking and the

happiness, Rich and I was full of love. His hands on my body, his lips on my neck, it made everything crazy, sexy and loving all at the same time. We enjoyed our bodies with clothes. At some point he asked me if we can go to a hotel in Manhattan. I agree with him and then I asked him to come over to my apartment.

"Sophie, we work together and the company does not accept relationships between employees. So, what will happen tonight will be just between us and it cannot repeat."

"That's fine Rich... We are adults and it will be just for a night."

I am so excited to enjoy Rich's body. He is so sexy and I want to love him tonight. I don't care about tomorrow. I just want to be with him tonight.

We landed on the edge of the yacht in a dark place. He leaned his body against mine, that I could feel his heartbeat and his rigid penis on my body made me almost moan. I don't know what happened with me. I just felt wild. I wanted him, at least for then.

We stop in front of my apartment and he asked me again if I want to do this: have sex with him. I nod. I didn't want to look like a girl who didn't know what she wanted.

We got in the apartment and he loves the place.

I opened a bottle of wine and I bring him a glass. We have a sip of wine. We look into each other's eyes for a long time. In my head I totally was for him. He made the first move, he grabbed my face and kissed me. His hand touched my hair, kissed my face, my neck, my bust. He slowly opened every button on my blouse. His hands gently touched my breasts. At first, I felt crazy but it was filled with pleasure, his confidence turned me on. Then he lowered his lips to my breast and took them with such will and pleasure that it left me very wet.

In this moment, I was so excited. My body craving his. My heart beats faster and faster. Where his hands touched my body, my skin shivered.

I laid down on the sofa. We kissed each other so much. His eyes were so into my eyes that I can feel his soul. He took off my panties and opened my legs. I couldn't believe I had so much pleasure like this. I held his head between my legs and he made me so wet, it was so hot that I could give him everything from me. My body, my love, my everything.

He pulled me up on his body, and finally I felt him inside of me. It was so wonderful. It was very good and special. His mouth delighting my breast, his hands firmly hold my body against his body. We love each other fervently. It was an amazing night. After a long time we got exhausted. I was fulfilled and relaxed and filled with such a love for this man.

I laid down on his chest. I fell asleep.

22 CHAPTER

Next morning, I woke up and Rich was in the shower. I was tired and I wanted to sleep more. Rich came from the shower and he was drying his hair. He is very sexy man.

He set down in the bed and talked to me about last night:

"Sophie, I'm sorry if I pushed you into this... it was amazing last night but now I am feeling guilty about it."

"Rich, I am a grown woman and I can decide about my actions. What happened last night was just last occasional sex."

I am lying. I wanted to say that last night was

full of love. It was very special for me and if we could repeat it again, I will love to do so.

"Great Sophie! The company philosophy it is that employees can't have relationship... We can be fired from there... I hope you can understand it."

"Sure Rich, I understood it at first place when you told me."

"I need to go... see you later."

He just give me a kiss on my forehead and left.

It was seven o'clock in the morning and I needed to be in work at eleven.

I just had a long deep breath, kind sadness. Inside me, I felt used or something, but I am happy that I will see him again in a couple hours. And it relieves me. I am already missing him.

At ten thirty, I was in the office. I have a meeting with a client and it is a very important meeting.

I pass by Rich's office and it was empty. After a meeting, that was around noon and the Rich office continue empty. Where Rich was today?

I went to the receptionist and I asked her what time Rich will be back at the office.

"Mrs. Sophie, Mr. Richard did not come into

the office today. He is receiving the calls on his cell phone. He has an emergency in his home."

"Oh ok."

"Do you want me to call him?"

"No, of course no. I can talk to him tomorrow. It is not important. It can wait till tomorrow. Anyways, thank you!"

"You are welcome Mrs. Sophie! If you need anything let me know."

"Sure, I will."

I went back to my office and I began to study my cases. Around six, I decided to leave for home. No sign of Rich. The office was busy, today, he didn't show up.

I got home. I wish I was going to call Rich and find out if everything was okay with him. He never misses a day of work and today he disappeared. But I never called him.

Like every night, I open a bottle of wine, call for delivery food and study my cases. At least today it will be Japanese food. But, right now I feel something different: I miss Rich very much. Like, I want to talk about my day and what's going on and make love with him later. But I will not text him. He will think that I am a young girl that falls in love with her boss...I guess it is my case.

My mom texted me and ask how the party was last night and I am with a naughty face answered her that the party was great.

My dinner got delivered and one more night by myself enjoy the food and my cases.

After a couple days, I even do not exchange a word with Rich. His office was filled up with meeting and people from California and Chicago and it never ends.

Just one morning we can exchange glances through the glass of his room, and that was it. The cases and cases didn't end. They just kept coming. I was very busy and it consumed me a lot of the time. One day I went to Rich's office and told him that I have a lot of cases and I was behind on it. He just turned to me and said:

"Hire someone to help you. I know we are getting very busy. Call at the department of Human Resources and find someone to help you as soon as possible. We can't be behind in those cases."

He turned back in his computer and it was as if he did not know me. It looks like he forgot the we had a fucking good night. I got sad when he didn't make any gesture of to me. Not even a smile. Well, looks like that was just one night.

23 CHAPTER

Mr. Philip called me and asked if I could come to California for help with some cases. The plane would be at JFK around ten o'clock at night. Well, I did not visit my parents for months and it is because how busy I was. I have a great salary, but I don't have time to spend time with myself. After a long day of work, I need to study cases in my home.

Around nine thirty at night I arrive at JFK and I went directly to the airplane as always. I was exhausted and I asked for a dinner on the flight. My salad and fish came. I also asked for some wine. I needed to relax. In a couple of minutes Rich also got on the airplane. I did not even imagine that Rich will be in the flight. I felt butterflies in my stomach and my heart beating faster every time and I saw him. I don't know what to say. After almost a month and a half, we were very busy and we never get a chance to talk again.

"Hey Sophie! Thank you for coming to help out the office in California!"

"No problem Rich." I answered, but I wanted to know if I had any chance to not go…

I open one of the file cases from California and I did not pay attention to Rich. I was nervous, but I tried my best to avoid him.

He asks for diner and tried to talk to me.

"Sophie, I am sorry for being very busy in those days. I mean, after us in your apartment."

I felt happy that he said that, but after such a long time… Why now? Maybe because we have a chance to sleep together again.

"That's fine Rich. I was very busy too…"

"I saw it. And you are doing a great job at the office Sophie. The owners are very happy with you."

"Thanks."

I was kind of cold with him, but my heart jumped so fast that I could barely breathe. He is such a handsome man. I want to stop the work and jump on him, kiss this man so badly.

"Do you think is possible that tomorrow, we can have lunch together Sophie? How long you will be in California?"

"I will be in California for just about a week..."

"Can we have lunch tomorrow?"

"I don't know Rich! Maybe..."

"Ok..."

He ate his diner and fell asleep. I continued to work and I would sometimes look at him. I like this guy. I want to be with him. I feel super attracted to him, by the voice, by the smell, by the sex. He would be the guy who I would probably like to share my life with.

The night we spent together he made me feel like a woman, and sexually desired by him. I can understand why he did not exchange a word with me after all.

If I have lunch with him tomorrow, I am scared that I'll end up in bed with him. If it's just sex, I don't want to be involved, but if he wants to share another type of relationship, I would go with him.

I am unable to maintain a sexual relationship with this man. I would quickly fall in love with him and I do not see him being into me.

We arrive at Los Angeles late. I was exhausted and I just wanted to get to the hotel. The driver was waiting for me and Rich.

I was quiet and I did not want to talk to Rich. When we arrived at the hotel, I took my bag and went inside to check-in my reservation. When I got to the elevator, I could hear Rich almost screaming across the hotel

"Sophie, I'll see you at lunch tomorrow?"

The elevator doors closed before I could answer his question.

I was confused about him and the only thing that I certainly knew was that I needed to focus on my job.

I got in the room, took a shower and went straight to the bed. I wake up next morning around seven thirty. I am tired, but I can do it. Another shower to wake me up and one coffee will refresh my soul.

I took a taxi and went to the office. There were a lot of meetings waiting for me.

Work, work and work. I did not see Rich around, but no time to think about it. Meetings, more meetings and work, more work… Gosh!

Mr. Philip came to me and asked if I want to diner in his home, and I said that it would be lovely.
"Sophie, I will send the driver to pick you up around nine!"

"Sure, thank you Mr. Philip."

24 CHAPTER

After a hard day of work, I left for the day. I looked at my cell phone and I saw some messages. Some from the NY office and my mom. The driver was waiting for me at the parking lot and I loved him so much for it. My feet were in so much pain because of my high heels. I am tired.

"How was your day Ms. Sophie?"

"Hi, well it was a very long day, but also, very productive."

"Good! Do you want to stop anywhere, or do you want to go straight to the hotel Ms. Sophie?"

"Can you stop at the mall nearby? I need to

buy a dress for tonight's dinner at Mr. Philip's home."

 "Sure! We have a small one next to us. And they might have some options that you may like."

"Great! Thank you very much! It is my second time being in Los Angeles. I forgot you name. Sorry, but what is your name?"

"My name is Jeff, Ms. Sophie."

"Thank you very much Jeff…"

The first store that I stopped by I found one black dress. It was not too sexy, but elegant and simple.

After buying the dress, I went back to the hotel, opened a bottle of wine and relaxed a bit, I really needed it.

I am crazy busy, but I have time to think about Richard: Where was he, or what was he doing? I put some music on my iPad. I played some pop music, it's more fun.

My phone make a noise, the one where you get a text. I thought it was my mom, but no, it was Rich, asking me if I was going to the diner at Philip's home. I just answered *yes*.

I know we will get together at some point. I just hope we don't sleep together again, but my hope is sleep with him tonight...God just help me...

I left my room and I meet Rich in the Hotel lobby.

"Wow Sophie! You look amazing!"

"Thank you, Rich!"

He was perfectly dressed; he was very sexy. A handsome man, as always, but I will not be telling it to him

The driver was waiting for us in front of the Hotel...

"Good evening Mr. Harris and Mrs. Johnson.

"Good evening, Jeff! Did you see how beautiful Ms. Johnson Sophie is?"

"She is always elegant!"

"Thank you, guys, this made my night." I joked.

Richard did not take his eyes from me. He talked to me about the meeting and how it was, and how things are changing here in Los Angeles's office because me and him.

"Rich, I saw that they are very behind on their cases and some files are not adequate. they need more organization and responsibility on it."

"Yes, Sophie, you are right! We will change the manager tomorrow. Philip fired him today. We will promote a good employee and see how it will work. But, know let's celebrate. Right Jeff?"

"Of course, Mr. Richard."

Rich was happy tonight. Normally he is stressed out, but he is enjoying this night.

We arrive at Mr. Philip's home and the simple dinner looks like more of a party. A lot of people were around and his home it is incredibly beautiful. Mansion.

Rich and I walk in the home front door. The front yard is amazing and everything looks perfect in the house. I really enjoy the cascade and the palm trees. The pool is in the front of the home and it looks fantastic. We got inside the home and Philip and his wife were there welcoming the guests.

"Nice to see you guys again. Thank you for coming."

"Thank you for the invitation Mr. Philip."

"Welcome Sophie. This is my wife Gabriela."

"Nice to meet you Mrs. Gabriela!"

"Nice to meet you too, Sophie. I am hearing

about the amazing job that you are doing in the office.   Congratulations!"

"Wow, thank you and it is great to hear that"

"Hello Rich! How is Allyson doing?"

"Hello Gabriela, she is fine… thanks for asking."

In this time Rich wanted to show me the house and looks like he wants to avoid the conversation.

"If you don't mind, Gabriela, I want to show Sophie the back yard and how it is beautiful."

"Of course, Rich, please, show it to Sophie…"

When we were going to the back yard, we heard Mr. Philip say to us:

"Both of you will receive a raise and a good bonus check for a couple weeks. You guys are helping us a lot around here."

"Thank you very much Mr. Philip!" I said.

"I appreciate it Philip." Rich replied to Philip.

I hold Rich's arm to express my happiness. While we were walking to the backyard Rich grabbed two glasses of wine.

"Working for Philip and Paul it is very good. You need to work a lot, sometimes no breaks, but the money is very good."

"How long did you work with them?"

"For about fourteen years."

When we got outside of the home, I was surprised: They have one band playing there and a big space to dance. Very well decorated and a lot of beautiful people, a lot of food and drinks.

"So, what time do we need to be in the office tomorrow, Rich?"

"I need to be there around nine o'clock at morning..."

"I don't even know what time I need to be there, but I want dance today. Do you?"

"Of course, Sophie, let's go to dance!"

We put our glasses on a table and we ran to the dance floor. Songs from the seventies were playing.

The lights, the palm trees, the music and the all energy around us, made me feel so comfortable to be with Rich.

After a couple songs, we stopped dancing and we went to drink a little more. We were sitting down at one of the tables and we started to talk about us, about our dreams and about our job. For the first time I've seen Rich express himself, complain about something or even talk about music or movies. He smiled a lot and I felt so fascinated by it.

"Sophie, I want to say something. Maybe it is not a good time but I hope you can understand it."

"You can tell me Rich, what it is?"

He looks uncomfortable in the chair, took a sip of wine and look into my eyes and said"

"I did not contact you after the night we made love, because I was scared. I was and I am scared, because our connection during that night was more intense than what I expected."

Now I took a sip of wine. My face was red and I did not know what to say. I took another sip of wine. He still looking into my eyes, my face, my hair. He was there just for me. He was just pay attention on me. I was also confused and scared about what will happen after this conversation. But I am ultimately happy.

"Also, Sophie I don't know nothing about you or your life. I try to keep that night behind us. But I can't take you from my head. I feel happy when I see you in your office and just seeing you make me happy."

I was so in shock… I just finished my glass of wine in two minutes.

"Well Rich, for me it was just that night like

we agreed if it. That night was an explosion of love and sex but was just that."

What was I saying? Am I being crazy or what? I want to say that I am in love for him and I want to be with him… but I guess I am confident about myself, after he say those words. And he made feel terrible for these past couple weeks.

He asked me to go around the yards and take more wine for us. We stop at in the corner of the home to take more wine and we walk and talk about the office in Los Angeles.

25 CHAPTER

Rich stopped in the dark spot of the front yard and held my face and kissed me....

This kiss brought me a wildfire that had been kept since that night of love and sex. His hand going under my bra and touched my nipple and he kissed my neck. I already was wet. I touch his penis that was very hard. His face went down my legs, he lifted my dress, lowered my panties and he licked me deliciously. OMG, I can die right now. This man can control my everything... It is so good.

Someone called his name from the backyard and we got daunt.

He says to me that he will see what is going on. I try to fix my dress and my face and I went to the front door. I went to the bathroom just to make sure my makeup was still good. I stayed in the bathroom for about fifteen minutes. When I leave there, I saw Rich with Mr. Philip talking in the back door of the house. They are laughing and having some fun. I took another glass of wine and I walk into the home. It had so many paintings. Many pictures, there were very enjoyable. I spend long time appreciating those arts and pictures.

"Hey Sophie, I was looking for you!"

"Hi Rich, I was around here enjoying the paintings."

"The dinner is already served, let's go?"

"Sure."

"Sophie, you drive me crazy. I love being with you. You are hot and sexy…" He whispered

I smile for him and we walked into the dining room.

Everyone at the table was talking and me and Rich just look to each other like we're hiding our love… it was so fun, playing around… but we wanted to leave very soon… we want to go to the hotel.

I got in the driver's car and Jeff asked us how the party was and Rich answered that was amazing. He touches his foot in my legs and smile to me with a dirty face. We exchange a couple of words with Jeff and we arrive at the hotel.

At the hotel, the receptionist called Rich saying he has a message. He asked me to wait in the room.

I got into my hotel room and I go check my face.

He took around fifteen minutes to get in my room. I open the door and he gave me a hug and then he kissed me on my lips and it was a delicious kiss.

We make love all night long. I don't know, but he had an energy that destroyed me in the bed. After our crazy night of love and wild sex, we slept together. He hugged me while he was sleeping and it made me so happy and comfortable.

Rich looks like an angel and I am feeling like I am in love with him… definitely, I am in love with Rich. My confusion mixed of his power, our sex and delicious secret made a fantasy that I always wished for myself: this strong man.

I wake up around seven thirty, some noise woke me up and I was tired and I want to sleep more. I listened Rich in the shower. Someone rang the bedroom doorbell and Rich shouted it from the bathroom that it was our breakfast. I couldn't believe that he called a breakfast to us.

I opened the door and received a table with a very nice breakfast. I said thank you to the waiter. Rich left the shower and give a kiss in my mouth and hug. I hugged him back and I felt his penis very hard and I went down and I put my mouth on it. We have sex again, but this time, it was different, we kissed each other more and more.

We make love slowly, and his movements were softer… he was enjoying my body… and of course I was enjoying his as well.

"Sophie, you are a delicious woman. I love being with you."

"Please, don't stop please…"

I had so many orgasms. He made me scream twice. I try to control myself but looks like I can't do it.

26 CHAPTER

After we are done, we have breakfast together. It was so romantic and I was living a dream... I talked about the party and the other lawyers that was in the party.

He is dressing up and I looked at him. His body is in good shape. Just muscly. He is a really hot man.

When he left, he kissed me and asked me:

"Sophie, I need to go. Can we have dinner tonight?"

"Sure Rich, we can."

"So, see you later and try to be a good girl tonight, ok?"

"Ok… I will try it!"

I got in the office at ten thirty. Today was not that crazy busy. I have a couple meetings and I needed to talk to Mr. Philip. He asked me how the tax department was doing and I told him after my evaluation and meeting with people I already told them what to do about it. They are behind on the files and cases because of disorganization and it is unacceptable. Also, I said the small things left behind make a huge difference on all the tax cases process.

"I am impressed with you Sophie! You are very young but is a very smart lawyer. You have a great career in the future."

"Thank you, Mr. Philip! Tomorrow, I will go to the court to orient our lawyer with a good argument to win the case."

"Excellent! When you will be back to NY?"

"I believe Friday Mr. Philip."

"Ok, let me know when you return for sure please."

"Of course, I will."

Between my mom and the office in NY, my phone never stopped ringing.

When I returned to my desk, I saw one red rose and one small note: "Miss you!" I smile and felt so happy. I am happy because he is thinking about me and I really appreciated it. I know our romance need to be kept in secret until we really decide to be together. For me that's fine. I hope Rich doesn't take that long to want to be with me and tell everyone about us. I wish it so badly.

"Hey baby!"

I get scared quick but, I looked back and it was Richard continuing call me baby. My face was serious and I look around us to see if someone listened to what he called me.

"Rich, be careful…"

"What time tonight, can I come to your room? I miss you so much!"

"I don't know if it is a good idea and can we talk about it in the hotel, please?"

"Sure… I am crazy to be with you…"

"Ok Rich, ok… talk to you later…"

"Did you finish the report from the tax department?"

"Not yet. I need to see the new lawyers in the court to see their performance…"

"Great, you're the best lawyer in the world."

I love to see Rich playing around me with the jokes, but it gets on my nerves. I don't want people to know about us yet. They talk too much and I can't damage my name and my reputation with Mr. Philip and Mr. Paul.

27 CHAPTER

For the last three nights Rich and I enjoy a lot. Besides just staying in bed making love, we also went to some shows in Las Vegas. We look like a good couple together and those days enjoying ourselves makes me feel so happy and wishing that Rich can get seriously about us.

In our last day in Los Angeles we will have a dinner at a nice restaurant. We will meet there at nine. We will have separate drivers because of the different locations we had to work today.

I dressed up very sexy. Nobody, that I know, will be around, so can make this night unforgettable.

When I arrived at the restaurant around nine thirty at night, Rich was already there.

He came to me when I entered the place, he was very handsome. He was dressed up very well and his cologne was magic. It was perfect.

"Wow Sophie, you look very beautiful this evening. Thank you for accepting my invitation for dinner."

"Thank you, Rich! This is a very nice restaurant. Thank you for the invitation."

We went back to the table and a bottle of champagne was there. He made me sit in one chair and with very much elegance sat down in the chair next to me.

He served me a glass of champagne and put a black velvet box in my front.

"Sophie, this is a small gift for you. Sharing this week with you made me very happy."

I was in shock with how much care I received from Rich. At first, I thought that he wanted to be with me. We can start dating. We can one day be engaged and marry one day. I don't know, but I am so in love with this guy. He gave the box and asked me to open it.

Very nervous, that I can tell my lips are dry. Before I opened it, I took a sip of the champagne from my glass and I started to open the box. My hands were shaking. I didn't want to show him that

I was nervous.

Carefully I opened the box and inside of it was a beautiful and expense diamond necklace… it surprised me. He wants something more. For sure. No one gives a very fancy gift to another person, without a feeling. A good feeling… I hope the name of this feeling is love.

"Oh my god Rich! It is a wonderful gift. Thank you very much! I love it so much."

He came to me and put the necklace on my neck. While he was putting it on my neck, he kissed my neck gently.

"Sophie, you are a beautiful woman. You made the necklace more beautiful yet."

He took my hands and kissed both, he was so romantic. I touched the necklace and I was in shock and happy at the same time. His smile, his words and the place make my night a dream. I can't believe that I am here with this man and get to share all my love with him. I hope Rich can talk to Philip and Paul about us and I hope it can't create a problem for me and Rich in the office. I know the policy in the company is that no one can have a romantic relationship between employees. I could be fired…

The music in the restaurant was very romantic. The band was playing piano ballads.

Richard and I start to talk about our job, from here and NY... he told me that he will make some changes in the office in NY... I want to talk to him about us. I want to ask him how we will be in NY and if he wants to us be a couple... but I can't do it... He just gave me a gift and I can pretend that I want to be his girlfriend.

His cell phone rang and Rich apologized to me and went far to answer the call. This was very strange of him. He never did that. I sipped my champagne and enjoyed the band playing. It was nice music.

"Sorry, Sophie. It was from my home and everything is fine."

"That's fine Rich."

This night was amazing. Richard and I had so much fun together. We exchanged ideas about our job, talked about old times, college times... but we did not talk about us.

We had a wonderful dinner, we danced to couple songs and we left to the hotel. Our flight was departing the next day around seven o'clock. I organized my things in the hotel and Rich called me and asked to watch a movie with him.

"Rich, just one second. I'm almost done here..."

"Sure, Sophie… I'll be waiting…"

After I organize everything I jumped in the bed and hugged Rich. We kiss and kiss and of course, we make love. I love enjoy Rich's body… His muscles are perfect and we make perfect love. I love this man…

We slept together again in my room. Around five o'clock in the morning we wake up. We have a shower together and get ready to leave. Jeff, the driver was there waiting for us… we stop at a Starbucks nearby the hotel to buy coffee that I love.

"Jeff? Do you want a cup of coffee?" I asked him.

"No, ma'am, thank you very much!"

Rich was acting different this morning. He was serious. There was no longer a smile on his face. He just grabbed his laptop and start to type. I ask him if everything was fine, he answered yes. He gave me a kiss and got back on the laptop.

We got inside of the jet and I took my laptop and start to check my schedule in the New York office. I open one email sent by Philip informing the I need to go with him to England next week. What???

"Rich, do you know that Philip wants me to go with him to England?"

"He told me yesterday, but I was not sure if he will call you to go. Normally, he ask Eva to go with him."

"Do you know what it is about it?"

"Yes, he goes to the University of Cambridge in the UK to do some workshops and inviting some of our employees to enjoy it. Maybe he will ask you to bring your presentation that you did into the Los Angeles office."

"All right, I guess…"

"Don't worry Sophie. This trip will be very important to your career."

Eva will kill me when she discovery that I am the one that will go to England. Anyways, why he is so weird today?

28 CHAPTER

During the flight back to NY, Rich and I just talk about the next meetings and some news clients that hire us.

"Be prepared Sophie... NY is busy."

"Rich, why are you acting like this?"

"Like what?"

"You are so serious and quiet..."

"Sorry, Sophie... It is just that so many things back home are already stressing me out."

"In your home?" I asked.

"Home, office, work... I guess everything. I

just want to say, Sophie, that those days together were the best days that I have had for a long time…"

So, let me think: that his words sound familiar to the words he told me when we had sex, at first time in my apartment. Now he is back to his life and I am just a part of his sex life?

I refuse to believe it! Is he using me or am I being precipitous in concluding his words?

I took a deep breath. I put my hand in my forehead. He is cold with me. He is not the same guy from yesterday… FUCK. I am in love with this man…

I got back to my laptop and I ask a cup of whisk for the flight attendant…

"Are you ok Sophie?"

I did not even look at Rich's face and I did not answer him. He noticed it but did not say a word. And it hurt… hurts a lot.

We got to New York and we went to the office. No words exchanged between me and Richard. I couldn't believe it.

In the office the receptionist welcome us and said:

"Mr. Richard, Mrs. Allisson ask you please call her when you get back in the office."

"Thank you, Helena. I will." Rich answer back.

Who is Alison? Philip's wife also asked about Allison. Maybe Allison is Rich's mother.

When I got to my office, I couldn't believe how many files were on my desk. All need to be signed…

So, on this "beautiful" day I got home after nine o 'clock at night. When I left the office, I saw Rich in his office with so many people. He looked into my eyes when he saw me stand by his door office. His eyes wanted to say something to me, but he turned his head to the meeting and continuing to talk to people there. It hurts again.

My apartment was very clean. My mom and Maria came from Connecticut to clean it for me. Even did my laundry. I love them so much!

I open my email and answered Mr. Philip that I will organize my schedule to go with him to England.

Two more new cases that I need to study for at least till Friday and I am behind with a couple cases also. Back to the NY life's back again: order

Japanese food to delivery and one glass of wine... and study and study.

I miss Rich so much. Maybe because I love him, but besides that I am very alone here in NY. I just go to work with no friends to go out.

I really want to understand Richard. He was so romantic with me and gave me a gift and now he is so cold. No, I can't not understand him at all. When we made love for the first time, it is ok that he wants to be far away from me, but in Los Angeles we enjoyed every day together. There was not just sex, we talked and went out all the times. We shared with each other dreams and plans for the future. Why is he acting like that...?

I open a bottle of wine and called for my dinner. I opened the first file to start to study the case when my cell phone ring... it was Rich...

"Hello!"

"Hello Sophie?"

"Yes, Richard!"

"Can I talk to you?

"Sure."

"Can I go to your apartment?"

I feel butterflies in my stomach. My legs shakes

because Rich asked to talk to me.

"Sure, I guess…" I said.

"I will be there in ten minutes."

"That's fine."

I am so happy, because he can explain to me why he's so distant. I took a sip of wine and I could not pay attention to my files. I stopped in my window at my living room and began to enjoy my view while Rich was on his way. Someone knocked on the door and I went to open the door. It was Richard.

He just hug me without any words and kiss me… and I can't be that strong to reject his kiss or his presence in my apartment. He start to open my blouse while we are kissing. His hand touch my nipples. If I was not wet, I would stop him, because I want to talk to him about us or about what's happened today. Why he was so cold with me. But I could not stop him. No… his hand went inside my pants and touched me delicately… his mouth went to my nipples and I do not have the power to stop him. I want this man inside me.

We make love in the middle of my living room. We did not talk, we just made love… delicious love, with so much pleasure. The delivery guy knocked on the door and we were in the most top of pleasure. We continue making love and delivery guy knocked for the second time. I said to Rich that I needed to get the door. I put my robe and run to open the door. The delivery guy gave me my order and left. I put my food in the kitchen and I came back to the arms to my love.

We have sex and love. It was wonderful.

"Sophie, I am sorry for today on the jet. I was stressed because I knew how much I need to fix here in NY and I was selfish."

"Rich, your attitude hurts me a lot. I did not know what to think about it. You were rude too."

"I am confused about us. At first, I thought I wanted just sex, casual sex between workers, but now I am missing you."

When Rich told me these words, it felt like I had life back in my soul. All my insecurity went away. I felt that he had to be telling me the truth. At this point the only thing I want is to be with him.

"I am confused too Rich. I want to be with you, but you are mysterious guy and I don't know how to deal with it. I don't know anything about you."

"I don't know anything about you Sophie. I just want to be with you and forget everything around us."

We kissed each other, but I could tell that Rich

was kind of stressed out.

"Let's go eat. I ordered Japanese."

"I love Japanese food." He said.

While I put plates and napkins in the table, Rich went to the bathroom. When he came back from the bathroom, he hugged me from behind and kissed my neck. We are like a couple and I love it.

"Do you want sleep here tonight?"

"I can't Sophie. I need to go home and see how things are going there."

"That's fine Rich!"

We have dinner together. We talk and I see Richard smile again and looks happy.

He helps me to organize the kitchen and wash the plates and glasses.

"So, I need to go…"

"I wish you could stay longer, but that's fine."

"See you tomorrow Sophie."

"See you tomorrow Rich."

We kiss each other and he left. Wow, I want he stay forever…

I showered and went to bed. I couldn't sleep

just remembering Rich words to me and thinking how my mom will be happy to know him…

29 CHAPTER

Got to the office at eleven o'clock in the morning. Just opened my email when Eva came to my office like a hurricane…

"Look Sophie, just because you are fucking Richard, you think you can get on the top of everything. Every year it's me that accompany Philip to UK and now you come here with this angel face and it messes up everything…"

"Wait Eva! I am not fucking with no one here at first, second I did not ask to go to UK with Philip."

I was in shock at this conversation with Eva… How'd she know about me and Richard.

"Everyone in this office knows about you and Richard, and it is not good for your reputation Mrs. Angel, and you are crossing the lines around here. Just be careful."

"Do not talk to me like that Eva. You don't know about anything… shut your mouth and get out of my office!"

"You are a fucking skank, Sophie. I am so sorry for you, it's absolutely pathetic."

Eva left my office and hit the door. My hands were shaking. I never fought before… What is going on here?

I went to Rich office but he was not there… I ask the receptionist Helena what time Richard will be in the office and she said that he will not come to work today.

I take courage to send one text message to Rich and ask him if he will come today to the office because I need to talk to him. He takes a while to answer me…

"Hello Sophie, no, I will not be going to the office today. It is everything ok?"

"That's fine, I will talk to you tomorrow."

"See you tomorrow." Rich reply me.

Talking to Rich made me calm down a little bit.

For the first time I text Rich with a personal issue. I needed to inform him about what Eva said about us.

I went back to my office and start work. Even when I try to concentrate on my job, but I could not stop to think what Eva told me earlier today. How did those people know about me and Richard?

Philip emailed me about the trip to England. I guess everything is all set. He also asked me to bring my Tax Presentation.

Very busy day with meetings and courts and left to my home around eight o'clock at night. I am so exhausted today. I walk to my home every day and I enjoy seeing how the city is busy: lots of people and lights that make me happy. If I had some friends, I could go to a bar tonight. I will not work today at home. Enough for today. I sat down on a bench for a little while and began to think about my life. I am happy for my choice to come to work in NY and everything looks like going well for me.

I never see the amount of money in my bank account. It is a lot of money and I don't have time to spend it. And in the middle of my choice I meet this guy. Richard made me dream of a serious relationship and one day to get married. Someone to share good or bad times with someone. Being with Richard made me relax and make me happy. I think

I love this man.

My mom texted me and ask if everything was ok and I text her back yes… maybe before I go to UK, I can go to Long Island and see my parents. But this is the only free time for me and Rich to be together before the trip. I don't know.

30 CHAPTER

I decided to stop at a bar and have a beer and a dinner there. I am alone but at least I have a lot of people around me. This bar is a very nice place, kind of dark but it has a lot of charm. I sat down in the bar and the bartender was super cool. While I was drinking and eating, he came back to me and we exchange some ideas. At least I have a great company tonight.

To my surprise, Richard texted me and it made me very nervous.

"Hi Sophie, can I pass by to your apartment? Are you home?"

"Hi Richard! No, I am close to my home. Just eating and getting a drink… Do you want to come over?"

"Nice… can we meet in your apt?"

"Sure, I will be there in thirty minutes." I said.

"Perfect! I will be there in forty minutes."

"Great, see you there."

I am very happy right now.

"Hey my friend! Can I have the check please?"

"Sure! Do you one more beer? It will be on me?"

"No, no, I need to go. Next time I will accept it!"

"Ok, next time!"

I want to run to my home and have a good shower before Rich get to my apt. So, I did. I was a few blocks away from my house, so I ran. After a relaxing shower and feel so good, I put one comfortable cloth, a nice perfume and I open a bottle of wine. It took him more than an hour to get there. I almost fell asleep on the couch.

The bell ranging and I went to open the door. He was there so handsome with flowers in his hands.

"I am sorry to get here this late. The traffic was horrible. I am sorry. This is for you."

"That is fine Rich... OMG, these flowers are

very beautiful… Thank you Richard, I love it."

We kissed for a very long time and we hug each other so romantic. I asked if he wanted a glass of wine and he said that he did.

I went to put the flowers in the vase.

We sat down on the sofa in the living room and we look to each other into our eyes. He smiled and we kissed again. He took a sip of wine and said to me:

"I really missed you today Sophie. I was busy, but I couldn't take you off my mind."

"Wow, you are so sweet saying this for me."

And kissed again and we make love on the sofa. Always is amazing feeling Rich's body weight on top of me. Feel him whisper in my ears that he loves making love with me and see him feeling pleasure is magic. His movements when we have sex is grateful to me. He makes me feel like a woman.

I really want this man to myself, forever. He did not sleep at home that night. I asked him to sleep with me but he said that he can't…

I started to imagine when he will be in my bed with me every night. Rich is so romantic and kind. Spending time with him is precious for me. I did not mention about what Eva told about us today in the office. I wanted to enjoy my time with him, and I didn't want to cause any problems. Tomorrow I will talk to him about this matter.

I wish I could convince him to be here tonight. But I couldn't... maybe next time... maybe next night.

31 CHAPTER

I got in the office early next morning. Around nine o'clock in the morning I got there. I ask Helena, the receptionist, if Richard was in his office and she answered yes, he was.

"Could you please, ask if he can talk to me right now?"

"Sure, Sophie, of course I can, but I don't think is necessary to inform him that you want to talk to him."

"Why not? He is my boss and please, ask him."

"Mr. Harris, Sophie would like to know if she can talk to you right now? Ok. Ok. I will let her know. No problem. Thank you, Mr. Harris."

"Can I go in his office?"

"Sophie, he asked if you can go talk to him around ten o'clock. He is in one meeting right now."

"Ok, no problem. Thank you."

"You're welcome."

What meeting did he have today early? I did not hear anything about it. I opened my office and I see one rose with one note saying: *"love being with you..."*

My heart bit faster and me smile. He is so cute.

I need to organize everything before my trip to the UK. So, I have so many files to sign and pass to my assistant to schedule an appointment with clients.

Very busy I was than I did not remember to talk to Richard at ten o'clock... he knocked on the door...

"Are you busy, Sophie?"

"Hey Richard, yes I am. Sorry, I did not pay attention on the clock that the time pass by and I did not have a chance to talk to you at ten."

"Ok, I was waiting for you. But, that's fine.

Can I help you with something?"

"Can you close the door, please?"

"What is going on Sophie?"

"Well, yesterday Eva came to my office very upset because I am going with Philip to UK."

"Eva is crazy lady. Don't worry about her. She is always upset with something…"

"But she said one thing very strange. She said that everyone in this office knows about our relationship."

"Hum… Sophie, just ignore her. Those people talk too much."

"Are you sure Richard?"

"Positively… So, are you ready for the trip?

"Yes, Richard, I am… All my cases are organized and I will be in contact with my assistant from there."

"Let's go to lunch today?"

"Sure, what time and where?"

"Around two o'clock in the afternoon at Palomino 5th Avenue."

"Ok, I will be there."

He left my office. I did not expect Richard to invite me to lunch today. I am very excited with this relationship with Rich. I never got that involved with someone like him. I love to share moments with him. I want to be with Rich all the time. This trip will calm me down a little bit. I need to put my head in control of my heart... I need focus in my career. I need to conquer my professional life first and later I can be involved like this. This guy makes me crazy...

Around one o'clock I left the office to go to the restaurant to meet Rich. I am so excited to meet him there and I want to talk to him about everything anything.

I need to stop in the post office to buy some stamps to send some postcards to Emma and Jerry, and after that I will go to the restaurant Palomino.

When I get there, everyone from the office was there. I thought that lunch was just for me and Richard. So, I was so happy for nothing. I have a pile of work and I don't even want to see Eva's face. Very disappointing.

We all have lunch together and Rich sat far away from me. I was the first to leave the restaurant. And I paid my bill and I went directly to my office.

I was very busy. I needed to organize my office here in NY before my trip to the UK with Philip.

While soon, Rich text me:

"Hey Sophie! Where are you?"

"I am in the office."

"Wow, I did not notice that you were left."

"I am busy and I need to do some important things before my trip."

"That's fine. See you later."

Perfect, after an hour he just notice that I was not at the restaurant. This shows how much he is paying attention on me. Let me get back on my work: sign document, petitions and more petitions.

I wish I can visit my parents before my trip, but I think it will be impossible.

32 CHAPTER

Today it is my trip. Everything is organized and I will not be going to work today. I need to go to the salon do my nails.

Rich and I exchanged a couple of text messages and that was all. I miss him so much and I want to be with him before I leave the country. Around twelve o'clock I missed a call from the office. I tried calling back but Helena, the receptionist didn't know who was trying calling me. In few minutes I received a text message from Rich.

"Hey Sophie! Are come to work today?"

"Hi Rich, not… I am not going to work today. Is there

a problem?"

"No, everything is fine. I was wondering if I could say goodbye to you."

"Ok, goodbye!"

"No Sophie. I mean, I want to see you."

"Well, I will be home around two o'clock…"

"Can I go in your apartment?"

"Yes, you can…"

"Ok, I will be there at two."

I really want to understand my relationship with Rich: I want to be with him so much and I think and believe he feels the same. Whenever we look at each other, it's always with second thoughts… even when we are in a meeting we look in each other's eyes more than necessary, we smile to each other, he touched my hands and much other things that couples doing when they are flirting… but, he has never demonstrated his serious intention for me. He never talks about dating or want to meet my family. We have been together for around four months and we just have sex. I love having sex with him, but I am missing another part of him. I want to share my time with Rich. Go to dinner or watch a movie together. I want to spend more time with him.

I get home and I left the door open. I went to the shower. I pretend that I forget the door open, while I have a shower, but it was intentional: I want to have a shower with him. I listen to him when he gets my apartment and he walked straight to my shower:

"Hello beautiful! Can I get into this shower with you?"

"Of course, boss!"

He got into my shower and we hug each other very strong. We kiss. This kiss made me realize that I really am in love with him. His hands touched all over my body. The soap made his hands slide easily across my body. He kissed my neck and turned me to the wall... and we had sex.

Looks like we never had sex before. We love being together. Our bodies were on fire. Our hearts were in love.

After our delicious shower, we went to bed to talk about us. He was kind and gentle and it made me so happy and confident that we will be happy one day. I was already missing him before the trip. He told me that when I come back from the UK, we should take a small trip to Hawaii for a couple days. I agreed with him... It would be a dream.

He helped with my lugged and he drove me to the JFK to take the plane. We kissed and he left.

I am in love with this guy and I can't resist him. While I was waiting for the plane, I texted my mom.

"Hi mom!"

"Hey baby! How are you?"

"I am fine, I am here in the JFK waiting for my plane. Mom, I need to say something…"

"What is happened baby?"

"Mom, I am in love!"

"Really, darling? That is awesome Sophie!!! Who is the lucky guy my love?"

"It is a guy from my job. We are dating, not seriously yet, but soon I will bring him to you guys. He is a nice man and I am in love."

"That is great news!!! Sophie, I am so happy for you and I am pretty sure your dad will be very happy too."

"Thanks mom… I am happy too. So, I need to go I will text you when I get in UK, ok? I love you."

"I love you too Sophie… Have a blessed trip!"

Philip just showed up and we went to have a couple drinks before the airplane took off. He explained to me how he is happy that I am going with him. I told him that I prepared my presentation better for the workshop and he thanked me.

33 CHAPTER

We got in the UK and we went straight to the hotel. We were tired from these six hours and a half hour of flying... I was exhausted. When I laid down on my bed, Rich text me asking if everything was ok and I say yes... Also, I text my mom too, saying that everything was all right.

Philip said that we will be in the next morning at the University of Cambridge around eleven o'clock in the morning to see the space for our presentation.

We have a couple hours of sleep. The time zone of five hours did not allow us to sleep well.

My alarm went off and I went to get a shower to help me out... my body needed to be in bed but I needed to go to work. I met Philip in the hotel lob around nine thirty in the morning, in London.

We have a fast break fast and we rented a car to go to the University of Cambridge. Philip explain to me how we will work in there. How we will do a presentation to the students and professors. We will work two days with three days apart and we have a chance to go around to visit some museums and other histories monuments.

"Thank you, Philip, for this opportunity to be here and participate with you in this workshop. Plus, we can go around we enjoy London."

"Sophie, if you are here it is because you work hard for it. You are very smart and professional. You help yourself. Keep it up."

"Thank you."

"You're welcome Sophie. Well, I have some ideas to us to visit some places. They are little far from London, but I believe it will be worth."

"Nice Philip! Which place do you think is good?"

"I want to go to the Tower of London and Roman Baths. They both are rich in architectural and history. Also, in the Tower of London we can have great food Brasserie Blanc, a fantastic French restaurant."

"Wow, I will love to visit it and enjoy the menu in the restaurant." I said.

"So, Sophie tomorrow it will be our first presentation. It will be at eleven o'clock in the morning. After we visit the University today, we can have a day off in the hotel and prepare for tomorrow and after tomorrow we can go visit the Tower of London."

"I completely agree with you Philip! I need to check out my presentation and sleep a little bit."

When we get in the University, I was impressed with the architecture of the University. Beautiful.

Rich texted me and ask with everything was ok and I answered yes.

"I miss you Sophie, more than I thought and more than I wish…"

"I miss you too Rich. How things are going in the office?"

"Everything is fine… Do you like London?"

"Yes, I do. I visited London when I was in high school. I love this place."

"Sophie, I miss being with you… I want to kiss you so

bad… When you get back in the States, I want to be with you in your apartment ok? Can I sleep over?"

"Sure Rich. Of course, you can… I told my mom about you. She wants to meet you."

"Wow, my mother in law wanted to meet me? I am nervous right now."

When Rich said "mother-in-law" I felt so happy. I cannot explain, but I felt security on our relationship. I needed much more with Rich. Not just casual sex. I want to be with him. I want to share my life with this guy.

"Yes Rich… When we have a chance to go to Greenwich, we can visit my parents."

"For sure Sophie! We will… So, enjoy your trip and talk to you soon."

"Talk to you soon…"

Philip show me the area for the presentation. It is a big classroom.

"Philip, how many students will be here tomorrow?"

"Well Sophie, around two hundred."

"Wow, it is a lot!"

"Are you scared?"

"No, I am not. I am very prepared for it. I am just surprised."

"Great!'

So, after we saw the place, we went back to the hotel. Philip and I went to lunch together and after that we went to sleep a little bit.

I get in my room and I check my messages from Rich. I look like an adolescent. I can feel the butterflies in my stomach. My heart jumps fast when I think of him. Rich make happy and I love being that way.

I took a shower and I decided to check my presentation for tomorrow. Everything is ok and I went to bed.

Wake up a couple hours later. The time zone confounded my brain and I cannot sleep well. I decided to walk around the hotel.

OMG, it is a beautiful place. It is a beautiful city. Stores and coffee places are very cozy. I decided to take one cup of tea and read a book. It was a small store book and very cozy place. I spent a while in there. I almost read the whole book. I check my clock. It was eight o'clock at night. I want text Rich a good night but there it is too late. I wish being there with Rich.

Finally, I got tired and go to the hotel is the

best decision for right now. I hope tonight, I will have a good night of sleep… I need it…

When I got the hotel, Philip was in the lob reading a newspaper.

"Hey Sophie! Were you around the city?"

"Yes, I was in the small bookstore nearby the hotel. Now I need to go to bed."

"Have a good night…"

"You too…"

When I got the elevator, my phone sounds and it was a message from Rich. It is late. It was a pic of him… almost naked… really? I smile to myself and I appreciate his body… he is a handsome man. OMG…and he writes: "sleep thinking of me… with love, Rich…" How I couldn't resist this guy. He is adorable, sexy and a lovely man. I just send back one heart to him… But what I want is to say that I am in love with him. I want to be with him forever.

I went to bed and dreamt with this angel.

34 CHAPTER

Wake up and feeling very happy to do the presentation. I hope I can do it well. Meet with Philip in the lobby to get breakfast and organize last updates for the workshop.

We arrived there at ten o'clock in the morning. I went to my classroom and I see a lot of students there already.

One employee from the university help me out with the PowerPoint and done. I was ready to talk...

I spent one hour in the workshop plus another hour answering questions from the students. During my presentation I saw Philip stand by the door and gave a thumbs up with a nice smile on his face.

Looks like he was happy.

I love being here. The students were so smart and very kind and I love the opportunity to share my professional experience with them. It was grateful. Also, I meet with professors that congratulated me for the presentation. I was proud of myself.

I meet with Philip in another classroom to watch presentation from a professor of this University...

It was a good time... being around with smart people is a gift... and I love it.

Rich text me almost five times, but I couldn't answer him.

After all the presentations that me and Philip need to be present for, we left. I was tired. It was around six o'clock in the afternoon.

Philip drive back to the hotel and I was texting Rich and my mom...

"Hi Rich. Sorry did not get back to you early. Very busy in the workshop..."

He did not answer me back. Maybe it is too late...

"So, Sophie, did you like it?"

"Wow, Philip! I love it so much… It was a very good experience for me. They liked my presentation and I felt very helpful to them."

"Yes, I love coming here. They pay us and we have a great time… so, tomorrow we can go visit the Tower of London… it will be an hour and twenty minutes from here. We can have lunch there and have a good time."

"Sure! I am excited for it!"

This night Philip invited me to dinner in a very nice restaurant to celebrate our positive result in the workshop. Rich and I texted each other all evening. For the first time I can assume the Rich is more kind with me. He is a gentleman, but right now he is romantic and we look alike a couple.

I meet Philip in the hotel's lobby around eight o'clock at night. He was talking to his wife. I can imagine being marriage to Rich. I don't know a lot about him, but at least our chemistry is really good.

"Let's go Sophie?"

"Sure."

"I was talking to my Gabriela, my wife. She already misses me."

"That is very nice to hear Philip… How long have you guys been married?"

"We've been married for twenty years."

"Wow! Long time. I presume you guys are very happy."

"Yes, we are. We have our differences but we know how to deal with them. I can say that I love my wife."

"Beautiful seeing couples in love. My parents are also married for a long time and they are very happy. I wish I can do great in my marriage."

While we are talking, we are getting a taxi to the restaurant. And Philip asked:

"Do you have a boyfriend Sophie?"

Good question, but I can say that I have. Because I don't even know my situation with Rich. Also, we are working in the same place and I don't want Philip knowing about my relationship with Rich... at least right now.

"Well, I am seeing one guy for four months and we have a good connection and I like to spend time around him. He makes me happy..."

"Great Sophie... I wish the best for you guys."

"Thank you, Philip!"

We got into the restaurant and we had a great time. We talked about the event that happened today and we also talk about the offices in NY and California. We drink wine and we have a blessed dinner.

Rich sent a message of "Good Night" and of course I answered back.

We returned to the Hotel around ten thirty at night and Philip said tomorrow around ten o'clock in the morning we should go to the Tower of London and I agreed with it.

I slept like an angel. I was tired and sleeping well was the medicine to my body.

Next morning, we had breakfast and we drove to visit the Tower of London. When we got there, after a one hour and twenty minutes, I was surprised with this historic castle. The castle is located on the North bank on the River Thames in central London… I believe it is the best attraction in London!

Walking through to the castle we can appreciate the rich history and so much to see within it. Beautiful!!!

We spent five hours there and we could have easily stayer longer. Wonderful experience.

"Sophie, I did a reservation in the very nice restaurant near here. It is call Brasserie Black. It is a French menu and the chef is a famous one:

Raymond Blank."

"Nice! I think I heard about him. His restaurant always is very required by the tourist."

"Yes, it is true."

We were tired of walking, but it was a very special moment to enjoy the history of London. Specially, because the castle was a resented symbol of oppression and built in 1078. Great time there.

We got to the restaurant and it was another spectacular experience. Philip order a bottle of wine. Again, we talk and talk. After a while we ordered our lunch. I asked for the Salmon & Mock Haddock fishcake, side of spinach and French fries and Philip ask for a Duck Leg Cassoulet… The Chief came to our table to bring the plates… it was very special… I am having a good time. After college I had time to enjoy other places like here and appreciate the foods. It looks like a vacation to me.

Also, Philip is a very good person to be around. Serious man but a nice guy to spend time together even besides working with it.

After our lunch we walked around the city. But we wanted to go back to the hotel. We need to check up again on our presentation for tomorrow and prepare for going back to the USA. I miss Rich so much. Maybe because I see him every day at work. I really want to go back home.

Issues

35 CHAPTER

It feels great to be back home. The professor at Cambridge University was very happy with our job. Also, we went to visit the Roman Baths and it was an excellent trip.

The driver from the office will pick me up at JFK. Philip took his private plane to go to California. He congratulated me for the great job that I did and left.

When I got to the exit to airplane I instead of seeing the driver from the office I saw Richard. I couldn't believe on it. He have a bouquet of flowers in his hands and a big smile on his face. I couldn't be that happy. I tried to organize my hair to it looks a little better and we hug each other and we kiss.

We kiss like two teens that are giving a loving kiss. Kiss that makes you feel lost in time, don't worry where you are, who is around… but the only and important thing in that moment it is that kiss, that love… that love that make the butterflies in our stomach jump.

Rich hug me so strong and hold me for almost a minute.

"Sophie, I missed you so much! I never thought that it will happen with me. I was counting the days until you come back home."

"I missed you too… yes I did miss you."

"Sophie, I did a reservation in the Japanese restaurant. Are you hungry?

"I think I am tired… Maybe we can have dinner in my apartment. What do you think?

"Sure, we can!"

We kiss each other again…

While we drive back to my apartment, I was telling Rich about the trip, the place that we visited in the UK, the presentation and the money I received from there. Also, I said that the trip was a great experience in my personal and career life.

He held my legs and was so attentive to me. He listened to everything that I said, kind of was enjoying listening to my adventures in UK.

When we arrived at my apartment, I saw my mom's car.

"Rich, I think my mom is here."

"Where Sophie?"

"In my apartment. This is her car?

"What now? I think is better I came back later."

"Maybe is time to you meeting her. What do you think?"

"I don't know…"

When we are talking my mom just say:

"Hey baby!!! I miss you! How was the trip?"

"Hey mom, hey Maria! What are you guys doing here?"

"We came to clean your apartment, do laundry and bring some groceries."

"Mom, thank you so much and thank for your love. You guys are angels in my life"

"So, Sophie…Who is this handsome guy?"

"Oh yes, this is Richard."

36 CHAPTER

Richard's face changed color… He looks so serious and uncomfortable to be introduced to my mom and Maria.

"Nice to meet you ladies. But I need to go. Sophie, I will see you tomorrow. She is tired the trip from UK is long and she needs sleep."

"I thought we will have dinner tonight."

"I think is better you enjoy your family and rest. You need it!"

Rich kissed my forehead, kissed my mom's hand and Maria's hand. And left. He even did not help with my baggage.

I felt so empty and I can't understand him. He literally do not want to meet my mom and run from us. What a waste is this… it broke my heart.

"So, mom lets go to dinner?

"Of course, my love. This is the guy that you told me about?"

"Yes, that was him…"

"He is a very handsome man and I already like him."

"He is a nice guy."

We put my baggage in my apartment and went to have dinner close to my home. We walked there.

While my mom talked to me, I just couldn't even pay attention to her words, for now I just wanted to understand the reason that Rich left. When we almost finish the dinner, I received a text message from Rich, saying he was sorry for the rude attitude today in the evening.

I actually, I do not want to accept his apology for his attitude. I am kind of mad at him. We had a great opportunity to talk and spend time with my mom and Rich merely threw it away. Plus, we can spend time together tonight, after all, we were away from each other for almost a week.

I am assuming by his innumerous text message, when I was away, that he was missing me, a lot… and then he just run away.

No, I will not be answering his text message.

My mom and Maria want to leave tonight. She doesn't like to leave my dad alone. I insisted to them to stay this night and leave early tomorrow. But my mom said "nope!"

That's fine, after all I needed to organize my luggage and have a good night to relax, because tomorrow I will be very busy in the office.

They left and I went to take a shower. I hear that someone was knocking on the door, probably was my mom… Maybe she forgot something…

"Wait mom! I am coming."

I told her while I wrapped myself in the towel. I saw around the living room and dining room and I don't see anything that belong to my mom… I opened the door saying, "mom what did you forget here?"

It was Richard…

37 CHAPTER

"Hi Sophie… "

"Hey, I thought it was my mom…"

He just hug me and kiss me without I agree or disagree with it…

My towel fell on the floor, but I really don't care at this moment. I just want Rich feeling my body warm and naked in his arms.

We slept together this night. What a beautiful night. This night was sealed with our love, our passion and our dreams. For the first time Rich told that he is in love with me and he wants to stay more often with me. I told him that I was reciprocated with that feeling and desire to be with him, to stay with him all the time... Also, I told him that I love him very much...

He asked me if we could go to one private island in Long Island this weekend and I agree...

We wake up and for me it was a dream. I wait for this time for so long and know I can be with this man.

"Rich, do you think Philip will cause a problem to know about us?"

"I am not sure about it Sophie. Give me time to figure out this situation ok?

We had a shower together and we change to go to work. Rich left first than me.

When I got in the office one bouquet of red flowers were there. The writing on the card said, "I love you! R."

It was Richard... He sent the flowers and he stopped behind me and said,

"The flowers are to add some color to your day princess."

"It is so beautiful. Thank you!"

"Today you are very busy in meetings ok Sophie? The manager from California is here to talk to you and you have a lot of cases to see... Good luck pretty girl."

"All right... Let's do this..."

So, all my day was very busy. Meetings and meetings, plus cases and mores cases, petitions and more petitions to sign.

All my week was very busy, it looks like everything was going well. Rich slept in my apartment three times already and I wish he'd move in over there. I would be so happy.

We will leave to the island Saturday morning. We will go there by boat. I am very excited with the direction is going my life. Great job, good money in my bank account, hope in a great future career and someone I love that I wish to be part of me for the rest of my life.

Rich is very comfortable with me. He shared his dreams with me and what he wants in his future.

I think it is a good sign once he puts me in his plans.

Another day, in my apartment, Rich was making a shake in the kitchen. I was studying a couple cases and I stop it to look on him. He cuts bananas, strawberry and avocado, put all fruits in the blender and waiting for it be done. All his movements are so hot and sexy. I love this guy so much; I love each perfect movement that he does.

There is a charm to the cooking, the walking and everything that Rich does. After he finished his smoothie, he came to me and kissed me. I believe we are doing very well as a couple. We respect each other, we are very kind and romantic with each other. The only thing that we did no resolved yet it is about how to inform Philip and Paul about our relationship. I am counting on Rich on this matter... I think I will be very uncomfortable to tell it to them. If they want, I can leave the office. I can find another job here in Manhattan. Rich worked in there for such a long time and it does not make sense for him to leave his job.

38 CHAPTER

Saturday morning, we wake up early to take the boat to go to the island. Rich said the island it is about one hour from Manhattan.

We had breakfast on the boat. Everything was very organized. The breakfast table was incredibly beautiful: flowers, fruits, juices, eggs and much more. We sat down around the table and enjoyed the food and the view. It feels great to be here with him. The view was very beautiful. Leaving Manhattan's building and going through the ocean it is perfect view. Richard looks very happy too.

"Baby, the island it is just for us. My friend traveled to China for a couple weeks and we are free to be there. I asked the lady that lives there to buy some groceries for us to cook tonight. What do you think?"

"Rich, I think that is perfect!"

"The weather it was not that good today, but we can at least relax from the busy city… I think you will love that place."

"I am loving it already. Thank you for this idea. Rich, I want you to consider the possibility of visiting my parents as soon as possible. I want them to meet with you and I think they will love you."

"Sure, Sophie! I will… I am just a little busy, but soon you can introduce me to your family. I promise."

We enjoy so much the small travel that we are having. After the breakfast we sat down on the chairs outside in the boat just to appreciate the beauty of the nature around us. We kissed each other a lot and we are in love. I can see that Richard it is not resisting me, my kiss or my body. He is in love with me, like I am in love for him. We are look like teenagers that are in love and can't be far away from each other.

The island is incredible…perfect… OMG, it is a paradise.

"OMG, Rich! It is amazing this place!"

"It is because you did not see inside. It is gorgeous…you will love it…

So, this weekend was amazing. Rich and I cooked, went to the beach, jet sky, kayaked, we had a blessed time together. I took in some sun and tanned… We relaxed a lot.

I loved to wake up in the morning and see his body laying down in my bed, his blue eyes looking inside my eyes, his voice kindly calling my name. His smell is my best breath of the day. It looks like a dream.

"Sophie, do you prefer leaving for Manhattan tonight or tomorrow morning?

"I prefer to be here, with you! I don't want to leave…"

We laugh, but we decided to leave on Monday morning. All this weekend was perfect, just one thing bothered me: two times Rich answered his phone and walked away from me. Literally, he spoke softly and walked away from me. It was weird, but I don't want to ask him who was in the phone. Normally, he'd just text, but this time someone called him and he answered immediately.

Besides that, everything was perfect! We had a great time together.

We wake up on Monday morning and we leave. Rich told that he loves and wants to be with me for a long time…. How I love hearing his voice saying lovely things to me…

39 CHAPTER

I began my week very busy. Tuesday, people from California are coming to NY and Philip and Paul want to do some changes that a lot people are involved. They want to close some small offices in Connecticut and Florida. I am exhausted, I am working a lot of hours with no extra payments. I really want to see where it will all be over. Poor Richard, he is the one that works crazy hours and looks like he needs to work more to finish his responsibilities...

Four hours of meeting, a lot of change, stress for everyone and some people were fired. Wow, crazy to see so many changes...

So, let's go... Like my father once said: "nothing is better than to be your own boss..." I agree with my dad.

Rich text me later asking if I want to go watch a show in Manhattan.

"What time Rich?"

"At eight. I bought the tickets already. Hamilton… It's a great show."

"Perfect! I'll see you there at seven forty-five at evening ok?

"Perfect! I'm missing you!"

"Are you sure, Rich, this is what you want to do? Today was a crazy busy day…"

"Sophie, every day is busy. Today was not different to me. So, see you soon baby."

"See you…"

I have a lot of things to finish before I leave the office today. Also, I had a plan to study some cases tonight, but I think I will do it tomorrow, because I want to have some time with my love.

We meet at the Theater Richard Rodgers at seven forty-five in the evening. We meet each other with a kiss and a lovely strong hug

I think Rich is more kind with me. We are having so many times together and we want to be together more and more times. When we got inside of the Theater, we seat in the front line with a great location.

"Sophie, I stopped today in one store and I saw one beautiful think like you."

He handle me a small box. Black small box. My heartbeat so fast that I could not speak one word. My mind just did this question; "is he proposing to me?" No, no, it is too early. Of course, if he does that, propose me, I will accept it. My eyes shine and my hands start to shake.

I put myself together and I took a deep breath and I open the box.

"Did you like it, baby"

"I love it Richard... it is very beautiful ring."

We kiss more and more after the gift. But it was not an engagement ring. I was so excited before, knowing that it was not one propose moment, I get a little frustrated. But, that's fine. It is to early anyways.

The show was spectacular!!! Hamilton is the most exciting and significant musical of the decade. This show makes me feel hopeful for the future of musical theater. Beautiful, beautiful, beautiful.

After almost three hours of the show, we got hungry. We decide to dinner at Trattoria Trecolori, an Italian restaurant. I went a couple times there and

I love it. Rich also likes Italian food. While we walk thru the restaurant, we enjoy walking in the City. I love to see people all over the place. The lights and shine of the building makes the Manhattan a great place to walk and have fun. Richard and I walked and held hands all the way to the restaurant. I believe that we are a couple. We are in love and I am very happy to enjoy these moments with Rich.

We sat in the table and the place was wonderful. We ask for wine and while we decide our dinner we talked about the show and how great it was. The performance was splendid and we love it. We laughed and remembered of the island how it was a good time and we are having a great time together.

After dinner we went to my apartment. I thought that Rich would sleep over but he says no. He needs to be home and he needs to go.

"Oh no please, sleep with me tonight. I can make you very happy… please, stay with me…"

We laugh and we kiss each other, but he left. I was so sad… I really wish that Richard could sleep with me tonight.

40 CHAPTER

My week was going well. My job was flowing well; Rich and I was very happy together… until I get this message from my brother:

"Hey Sophie! I wish not to inform it to you, but dad got in a car accident and he is in the hospital. I think is better you come home. Mom is very emotional and needs us."

"Robert??? Wait? It is dad ok? Please, I am very nervous right now. Please, tell me?"

"Sophie, I don't have any information about the dad's situation. I am sorry, but I just know he is in the hospital. Please, come home."

"Of course, I will go. I will take a train."

"The driver can pick you up in forty-five minutes. It is not that late and the traffic is not that bad this time of the day."

"Sure. Can he pick me up in my apartment? I will send the address."

"Ok."

OMG… I can't feel my legs right now. I can even breath… Ok, I need to put myself together and go home, takes some clothes, put it in a bag and calm down. I am really stressed…

"Hi Rich! I need go home."

"That is fine Sophie. But I think you don't need to inform it me to, right?"

"Not my home here, in NY. I need go to Greenwich. My dad got into a car accident. My brother just texted me about it."

"Are you ok, Sophie? Do you need the driver to take you home?'

"No, thank you. My brother already send our driver to pick me up."

"I am sorry Sophie to hear it. I hope that your dad is fine. Are you mom ok?"

"I don't know…"

Richard hug me. I am completely worried with

this news. He served me a glass of water.

"So, ok Sophie. I will help you to go to your apartment. Do you think it is fine?"

"I guess so… Thank you. The water helped me calm down a little bit."

"Let's go?"

"Yes, let's go."

When we left the office to my apartment, Rich told Helena, that he will be back in two hours.

"Anything for Sophie make a note. If it is important, contact me, please!"

"Sure, Mr. Richard."

I never felt like this. I am lost. It feels like I don't have any power to get in my home fast or know how is doing my father. It is the worst feeling ever.

41 CHAPTER

The driver arrived at my apartment and I left for Greenwich, Connecticut. I texted my brother to know if he had any news from the hospital. He did not answer me back.

"Hello Ms. Sophie. How long I did not see you!"

"Hello Javier… Yes, it is true. Living in the city is very busy. I am working hard and often have no time to go home. Do you know something about my dad?"

"No Ms. Sophie. Nobody knows anything yet. Your mom was very nervous and she left to the hospital early today."

"Where was my dad when the accident happened?"

"He went to Trumbull, Connecticut. When he

was returning to home one car hit him or something like that."

"Oh my God… I hope he is fine. I don't want to call my mom right now…"

"Calm down Ms. Sophie. Everything will be fine. Just pray… The traffic is not bad and we will be home soon… don't worry…"

How can I not worry? My dad it is in the hospital. While I was going to Connecticut, I was remembering how my dad and I played so much when I was young. He loved to run around with me and my brother. I love my dad so much that I can't imagine if something bad happened to him.

I decide to call my mom… and nothing… she also, did not answered. This drive back home is so long, never ending… ten minutes feels like an hour. Gosh calm me down, please…

Richard text me asking if I am was ok. I said yes, but my heart was in pain. I was scared if something happened with my dad.

My brother texted asking if I was on my way home and I said yes, that I was. I ask him about my dad and he text that they did not know yet what is going on.

42 CHAPTER

When I got in the hospital, I saw my mom. She was devastated. She was crying. When she saw me, she screamed my name out loud.

"Sophie… What happened with your dad my darling…"? I need to know now about him…" My heart is in pain …"

Wow… seeing my mom in that situation makes me feel more responsible for her feelings. If I cry, she will pass out…

"Mom, everything will be fine… mom…"

My mom, start falling… she was passing out… I call for a nurse that was in the hallway that help me out with my mom.

This situation is the worst one that someone can have it. I don't have power to control anything. In the middle of this confusion, my brother came and asked to come with him. We went to a small room.

"Sophie, dads it is not good. He is losing blood and they are trying to stop it. Also, he needs to go to a surgery any time from now. He broke some bones and one of the bones hit one vascular vein…"

"Oh my God!!! Robert is it possible he could die from it?"

"Yes, he can…"

"Oh no Robert!!!'

"Sophie, I think is better you don't tell it to mom right now. She is very stressed and she will make everything worse."

I sat down in one sofa in this small room. I couldn't cry… my throat got dry and I stayed quiet for a while. My brother sat down on another sofa in the same small room. I never saw my brother sad and worried like today. We looked at each other in silence… and the only and painful option that we have in that moment was wait.

Wait with patience… Just the hope and fear was in our feelings… my dad could die any time and we cannot do anything to change it.

43 CHAPTER

My mom woke up. She was tired of crying and being stressed too. The nurse gave a medication to my mom calm down.

We sat in silence for a while…

"I am so anxious Robert. Why we don't have anything from the doctors about your dad?"

"Mom, dad is in surgery room right now…"

"What??? Why???"

"Mom, mom??? Everything will be fine. Don't worry… just be patient, because we need to wait… just waiting…" I said to my mom.

"Sophie, thank you to be here in this difficult

time, my daughter."

"Of course, mom…"

I wish Richard could be here with me. Listen to his voice, make me feel more secure. He texted me two times already and I am so glad that he did that. It is very kind and gentle from him.

I asked my mom if she wants to go home to take a shower, change clothes and eat something. She agreed with it and we left.

"Robert, anything please, call us."

"Of course, I will."

"Robert, do you want something to eat? Maria is making soup to us."

"Yes, please Sophie. Thank you!"

"When I come from home you can go to your home and relax a little bit. Just take a shower…"

"Thank you, Sophie. Take care of our mother ok? She really needs it."

"Yes, I know it. I will and don't worry."

Javier was in the hospital waiting for us. He drove us home. My mom was very quiet and don't want to talk. Maria was outside home waiting for us. When my mom saw Maria she start, again, to cry.

Hard time it is. We felt powerless and wait for the doctor's answer in painful... it is scary...

My mom went to her room and I went to my room and I had a shower to refresh my mind, my soul and my everything. Richard called me while I was in the shower. I will call him later.

Maria call me to have dinner with my mom. I went downstairs. My mom was there in silence. I sat down and I put salad in my plate and a piece of bread. My mom just looked in the plate... her eyes were fixed on the plate...

"Mom, do you want salad?"

She looked at me... her eyes were in pain, she couldn't cry anymore, she did not have tears left...

"Why did this happen to us Sophie? Why?"

"I don't know mom. Things happened with everybody... I am sorry mom..."

"Your dad is a great man and he did not deserve it..."

"Mom, he will be fine. Eat a little bit. When he wakes up, he needs us strong to be by his side."

Maria was quiet there and put soup in my mom's plate. Also, put a piece of bread.

My mom thanked Maria for it and she started

to eat slowly. I asked Maria to prepare dinner for Robert to go.

"Mom I will go to the hospital, so Robert can come home and relax a little bit, ok? I think it is better you stay home with Maria and sleep. Tomorrow morning you can go to the hospital."

"I guess that is fine Sophie. Thank you, my daughter."

44 CHAPTER

I left my home and Javier drove me to the hospital. In all the middle of those feelings, I texted Richard just once and he texted more than five times. He asked me if I was fine and he wants to know how my dad are doing.

Javier tried to talk to me, but I really did not have any energy or attention to pay for his words. My mind is just thinking and worry about my dad. I already call the office in NY informing the Human Resources that I will be absent in the office for a couple days, also I give all directions to my assistant how to cover for those days that I will not be in the office. I don't want Richard calling me and asking questions about my cases. I was very surprised, because Philip sent a text message asking about my dad.

When I get in the hospital, Robert was sat down in one sofa in the waiting room. He was sleeping and I wake him up.

"Hey Rob!!! I brought some salad, soup and bread for you. Go eat and go home to have a shower and relax a little bit."

"Hey Sophie! Thank you! I took a nap and I am hungry too. How mom is doing? Is she feeling better? Did she stop to cry?"

He open the bag with the dinner and start to eat.

"Well, she is fine. I think she does not have tears left anymore. She is exhausted. Maria is there with her and I hope she can sleep a little bit."

"This soup is perfect!!"

"Did anyone bring some news about dad?"

"Just the nurse, informed that the surgery was almost done... but it was almost one hour ago. After her, nobody came to say anything."

"Well, we need patience and hope. My mind is lost Robert. I am so worried about dad. I am just thinking if something bad happened with our dad. Imagine mom, imagine us..."

After all day, some tears dropped from my eyes. I didn't want to cry, but my heart was so small and I was sad…. I am scared… I don't want to lose my dad.

Robert hugged me, kissed my forehead, and said:

"Don't cry, everything will be fine. Dad is a strong man and he will survive this accident. We need just be strong for him and for mom."

I dry my tears and I take a deep breath. We need to be strong in this hard time that our family is facing.

"So, go home Robert. Go relax and come back later…"

"Ok, I need to take a shower and change my clothes. Are you sure that you will be fine by yourself?"

"Sure, Robert! I will be fine."

45 CHAPTER

Robert came back home and I was waiting for some information from the doctors about my dad. I sat down in the waiting room when I saw Richard in the reception desk at the hospital.

OMG, I can't believe that he is here. Just saw Richard stopped at the front desk and probably asking about my family. Seeing him in the hospital made my soul alive again. I never thought that seeing him would make me feel strong, happy and full of hope. My heart jump faster and I walked in his direction.

The hospital receptionist pointed show the waiting room for him, but I was already going to his direction to meet him.

When he saw me in his direction, he came faster and faster and hug me… it was everything that I need in that moment. I was desperate waiting that hug.

"Are you ok Sophie?"

"Thank you for being here. It is a very difficult time for my family."

"I can imagine it baby. I am sorry for you and for your family…"

We kissed each other and we step outside of the hospital to take a break.

"How is your dad baby?"

"We do not know yet. We knew that he was in the surgery for hours but it was almost done. My dad broke some bones and lost a lot of blood… and other consequences that he needs the surgery. We don't know exactly how he is…"

"I am sorry baby… How is your mom?"

"She is not fine. Just crying and crying… She is home right now trying to sleep a little bit."

We sat down in one green space very calm outside of the hospital. It makes me feel with more hope and of course, Richard by my side, make my life easier.

"Sophie, I need come back home soon, baby. I am sorry, I wish that I can stay here more time with you and your family, but tomorrow we will have a meeting in the office with all offices manager and Philip and Paul will be there…"

"Sure, Rich! Of course, I understand it. I really appreciate your time with me here. It brings me so much energy to endure this time. Thank you."

We hug each other and it brought me so much peace. Being with Rich made me a better person, a better daughter, at long last, I am better in everything.

Rich spent one hour more with me in the hospital. The hospital took long to inform me that my dad it is in stable condition. Also, my dad went well in the surgery. The news gave me peace in my negative expectation about my dad. At least, dad is not in the intensive care anymore.

46 CHAPTER

My bother came back home and meet with Rich. They talk a little bit and Robert went inside in the hospital.

"Sophie, I need to go, ok?"

"Sure Rich. Have a safe trip back home please."

"I will baby. Say hi to your mom and I hope to meet her next time with your dad in better circumstances."

"Thank you, Rich… I will tell her."

Rich left and left my heart in pieces… I wish he can be with me till tomorrow. But that is fine. He already made my day. I was so grateful that he came here. I meet Robert inside of the hospital:

"Robert, dad is in stable conditions. He left the intensive care about two hours ago."

"Well, I think we can breathe right now, Sophie. Do you think we should call mom?"

"It is very late and if she calls us you can inform her and pick her up here."

"Good idea, Sophie."

Robert and I walk around the hospital and when we went back to the waiting room, I saw Richard wallet in one sofa.

I can't believe that he forget his wallet... It can cause him headache... Sucks. It is late, but I will call him and let him know that I have his wallet.

The phone rang three times and one woman answered my call. I just hung up, probably I called the wrong number.

Before I call again, my mom called me asking about my dad. I told her that he is doing fine and tomorrow morning she can come over. She wants come tonight and I asked Robert if he can go home and pick up mom to come to the hospital.

"Really Sophie? It is better she comes

tomorrow. I am tired to drive."

"That is fine. I will go."

I texted my mom saying:

"Ok mom, I will be there in fifteen minutes. Be ready ok?"

"Thank you, daughter, I love you."

"Love you mom."

I just said bye to Robert and I took Robert's car and drive in direction to my mom's home. While I drive, I used the speaker to call to Richard again. The same woman answer my called:

"Hello! Sorry, but it is Richard telephone number?" I asked.

"Hello, yes, it is."

"Oh ok, can I talk to him, please?"

"Sure, once second…"

I heard the lady's voice:

Lady's voice: *"Hey baby, someone called you… Baby? Richard? Hello, hold on, just a second please. I'll try to get him…"*

"Ok, thank you." I said…

I keep heard words that I could not believe.

My stomach get nauseous, because the words I heard make me sick. I stopped the car...

Lady's voice: *"Son, can you ask your dad to come here. Someone is calling him."*

 Kid's voice: *"dad is in the shower..."*

Lady's voice: *"Hello, whom is calling?"*

"My name is Sophie. Sorry to call that late, but it was kind urgent."

Lady's voice: *"That is fine, no problem at all. When he is available, I will tell him to call you."*

"With who am I speaking with?"

Lady's voice: *"I am Richard's wife, Allison."*

"Thank you so much Mrs. Allison. Have a good night."

Lady's voice: *"You're welcome Sophie, that is your name, right? have a good night. But it is everything ok with you?"*

"Yes, yes... it is just one client from the office and need some information. But I will call him tomorrow. Have a good night Mrs. Allison, have a good night."

47 CHAPTER

What is happening right now? Did I understand that right? Is Richard married? I open the car doors, I leaned on the car and took a deep breath, and I throw up.

My mind was confused and I even can't think it right. I am feeling sick, very sick. My thoughts right now remembered when Philip's wife ask about Allison, also, the receptionist in the office also mentioned Allison to Rich... I though Allison was his mother...

I cry out of pain. I cannot and do not want to believe it...

"AHHHHHHHH.... No, Richard, please, Richard, no... I could not believe that you are like this…"

I sat down in the floor outside Robert's car… I can't walk, I can't drive, I can't talk… The only thing I could do is cry… I threw up, my stomach was sick.

I stand up, holding in the car. I looked at the stars and the sky was clear. My tears cannot stop rolling in my face and I just need to put myself together and realize what just happened.

Cars passed by, the cold breezy hit my face. I get inside the car and I screamed… I screamed because of my pain, I screamed because I love Richard, I screamed because I hate him.

Should I call her again and telling her about her husband and me? Telling her what her husband are doing? If I do it, what's the difference in my situation? Can my pain go way? Or I want just hurt Richard and his family, right now? So many questions, and nothing will change it.

My mom texted me asking if I will pick her up her. I did not answer her. I could not…

My tears come down and I could not stop crying. My dream just broke down, the man I dreamed to build one family one day is already married. Worse than that, he never told me the truth. Why? Why and why?

After a while, thinking and remembering my moments with Rich, I took a deep breath and I could put myself together. I turned on the car and I drove to my mom's home. I stop the car and I texted her to come, because I was outside.

"Sophie, it is everything fine? Is your dad ok?"

"Yes mom, dad is fine."

"Why are you crying?"

"Mom, sorry, but I think it was too much emotion. Now that I know dad is fine, I guess I need to cry."

"Let's go inside Sophie. Drink water and relax a little bit."

"I will drive you to the hospital, mom, and I will go back here to rest."

"Yes, do it Sophie. What happened to your father it is really confusing and scary. I was thinking the worse with him. I could not control myself."

"Yes, I guess mom…"

My mom will never guess what happened with me. Besides, my dad accident, I discovered that my boyfriend is married. My heart is broken and I am lost. Completely lost. Why did Richard not try to reach me yet? He didn't even call me back. At least to explain this situation…

My mom went inside to the hospital and I drive back to my mom's home.

I went upstairs to my old room... I set down on the sofa and I start to cry again. I was checking all my message between Richard and me. How could Rich betray me and betray his wife? All his texts to me was lovely and kind. He never showed me that he had another life.

How many times he slept over in my apartment? We traveled together, we dreamed of a life together, we made plans... and now? What I will do with all those dreams? What I will do with all my life? I am in pieces... I am lost...

48 CHAPTER

It is almost three o'clock in the morning and I could not sleep, waiting Richard call me or text me. Nothing until in the morning. Around ten o'clock, I was already in the hospital when Rich texted me.

I just saw his name in my cell, but I did not read the message because the doctor was talking to me, my mom and my brother. But my stomach hurts when I saw Rich's name on my cell phone's screen. I didn't even pay attention to what the doctor was saying anymore. I start to think of what Richard would message me back. My heart was beating faster and I asked for an excuse to leave the waiting room.

My mom and my brother looked at me with a weird face, but I left the room. I wanted to breathe again, and it will just happen when I could talk to Richard. I can't wait for it anymore. This situation is killing me.

"Hello Sophie! Did you call me last night?"

This was the message Richard sent to me. What now? What do I say? I don't know. I am really lost. I don't know what to say to Richard. I am in pieces, and I realize it right now. I don't have words to talk to him. I am feeling like a stupid woman. I am in love with a married man and it will change everything. Maybe people in the office knew about us and knew that he was married. So, I am a mistress. Such a stupid girl I was? I can't think right now…

I went back to the waiting room and I continued listening to the doctor about my dad.

ONE WEEK LATER...

I decided to stay home with my family, I personally called Philip and explained my dad's situation and he agrees with me to take care of my dad. My dad is still in the hospital and we need to stay there. He will recover very slow but if I stay at least one week it will be fine.

Philip just remembered about the office party that will be next week, and it is very important for me to enjoy the party. And I can bring my boyfriend, if I want to. I confirm my presence in the party.

Richard sent the driver of the company to pick up his wallet. One morning the driver showed up in the hospital and ask for Richard wallet. Rich is so ridiculous. He realized that he forgot his wallet that day he came over to see me in the hospital and even did not ask me if I found the wallet or not. He just sent the driver to pick it up. Well, it is good for to me realize who he is…

49 CHAPTER

During this week in Connecticut with my family, I was realizing my life in New York. My career is going excellent and I love being working in there, but after what happened with me and Richard, I am not sure what I will do in the future.

I am not confident in myself that I will endure this situation with Richard with blood cold. I am still in love with him.

He did not call to me even once. Just sent a couple texts asking how I was and how was my father. To me, he was very professional while I think he should try to explain himself to me. He knows that I know that he is married. But, no words from him.

The worst part is when I close my eyes and I see his blue eyes, or when I remember ours great moments of love and joy that we had together.

When I closed my eyes, I see his eyes and it make hard to see…

My world is completely lost. I am alone and I can't talk about it with no one else. How can I tell my pain of love with someone is already married? It is a shame for me or for my family. My father will never imagine it.

I try to figure it out how I could not pay attention to the details, that should give me a tip, if he was married or not. No family's pics in his office, no married ring on his finger…

I remember once when Eva mentioned about Rich and me, I was mad with her, and the true was, she was trying to alert me, on how stupid I was being. Maybe she was trying to tell me that he is married or something. When he would answer mysterious phones calls, maybe I should've suspected.

I don't know what to do right now, I just know that I miss him so much. I miss his body, his smell, his smile, his eyes in my eyes. I miss him very much.

After my grudge, I am in pain. I need to put myself together, but I can't. At least for right now.

My dad had a good recovery after the surgery. He is doing very well, but the doctor needs him to stay in the hospital. My brother is covering my dad in the office and my mom and I stayed with my dad. I am glad that nothing bad happened with my dad. The car accident was bad but he is a strong guy.

50 CHAPTER

PARTY DAY

I really don't want to go to the party. My soul is dead and my shine is very dark. But, in this party they will give way a lot of gifts to all good employees, besides that, Philip wants to me to go. And everyone is excited about it.

I bought a nice and fancy dress for tonight's party and I went to a salon to do my hair and makeup. After all, in the end I am look very pretty woman with dead soul…

Richard never tried to contact me. It is causing me pain, because shows that he was using me for having fun with a young girl in the office. Maybe he commented about me with other guys that we were dating or fucking…

Also, he never tried to say sorry for his mistakes or because he is a jerk. Unfortunately, I am in love with him and anything that I do or thinks, leaves me alone with Richard's face. When I close my eyes, I see him and it makes it hard to see. I can't enjoy the blue sky, the busy Manhattan streets or the colors of the trees anymore... everything is gray like my heart.

I don't have any tears left to cry anymore, just the physical pain that I have to endure right now.

I took a taxi to go to the party. The party will be at OFFSITE Corporate 52W 39th Street. There is a great place to do a business party.

When I get there, everyone come to talk to me about my father and how he was. I explain to one by one what happened and how the car accident occurred, finally I was feeling a little better talking to people.

I saw Philip coming to me and of course he needs to know how my dad is doing.

"Hello Sophie! How are you? You are looking very beautiful tonight!"

"Hello Philip! Thank you!"

"How is your dad doing?"

"Philip, he is doing fine, thanks for asking. The party is amazing..."

"Yes, I like the good parties, especially for my coworkers."

While we are talking, people were walking around and the music was loud and I turned around to see if I can find Richard, when Philip call me"

"Sophie, did you meet Allison Harris before?"

When I turned to them, I thought my heart would stop in that exact time. It felt like I was blind and deaf. I could not hear the music; I could not see people around me. I was in shock; Richard's wife was there...

51 CHAPTER

"No, I haven't…" I said.

"Allison is Rich's wife, Sophie!"

"Hello Sophie, nice to meet you."

"Hello Allison, nice to meet you too."

"Allison is a great professional, she is book author." Philip said.

"Wow, how nice it is. Congrats. I hope one day I can read one of your books then." I said.

"Yes, you should Sophie. Allison is spectacular author. My wife and I personally read a lot of them and we love them."

"Thank you very much Philip. You made my night." Allison says.

"I definitely will read them."

"So, nice to meet you Sophie. I need to come back to my table. My kids are there and I don't want them to make any mess. Excuse me, please."

She went to her table and I saw Richard with two boys sat down in there. When she got to their table, I saw Richard push the seat for her and kissed her on the lips.

"They have children?" I asked to Philip.

"Yes, they have two boys: Lucca and Richard Junior."

"Richard never mentioned his kids to me, and we worked together for a long time…"

"Richard is very kind with his family. He will die for them. He loves his family."

"Yes, I can see… I need to go to the bedroom Philip…"

"Sure, your table it is close to Richard's table, in the left side ok?"

"Ok, thank you Philip."

I went straight to the bedroom. Couple people tried to stop me to talk, but I left them talking to themselves. My stomach hurts, I took a deep breath and I wanted to cry. How could Richard do this to me? How could he do that with his wife? She is a beautiful woman and very smart. He has a family… OMG, he has a family…

Philip started his speech and I went to find my table. I took one glass of wine, talked with a couple coworkers and I found my table. I did not turn my face to Richard's table. I kept watching Philip speaking. I even don't know what he was saying. My head was spinning. No logical thinking. I was shaking, then Philip call Richard to speak.

I saw Richard for the first time after everything happened. He started his speech and when he saw me, he turned his face away from my direction. What is going on. Now he is not a man to look into my eyes…or even look at my face...

52 CHAPTER

I left the party. I could not stand to stay there. Seeing Richard with his family gave me a sensation of lost my path in life. I want this man so much and I can't have him. I feel jealous of Richard with his family. He was so happy and grateful that I almost didn't recognize him. It was not my man.

I took a taxi. When I opened the door I start to cry, the driver asked if I was fine but I could not answer him. My world was falling apart. The driver kept asking if I was fine or if I need anything else, but I just told him:

"Please, go home, this is my address. Thank you!"

I got home with no hope of being better, but at

least I was far away from Richard. I lay down on the sofa. When I close my eyes, I can see Richard, or his wife or his kids.

I decided to open a bottle of wine. Maybe it can help me forget things that are impossible to forget. I have physical pain and it will not go away.

I put music, I drink, I cry, I laugh, but the only thing I need and want right now is to die…

After a while, my bottle of wine was almost done, someone knocked on my apartment's door. I was drunk and I don't want talk with nobody… door was knocked again and I hear a voice. It was Richard voice.

53 CHAPTER

When I heard Richard's voice in my apartment's door, I could not believe. Should I open it? Or want him to leave. Or do I need to hear his excuses... or I will hug him for the last time...

"Sophie, open the door. I know that you are there. Please, open the door Sophie. We need to talk..."

I am so sorry to myself, to be in love for this guy. If I open this door, what do I want to know? I already know the truth. But I needed to give myself a chance to understand why he did it to me. I am lying to myself. I want to open this door, because I want to see him again, to be close to him in our secret lies...

I open the door. He was there waiting. I look at his eyes and the silence took over the moment. No words could describe our feelings, our love, our fear of each other.

I turned around and I went back to my apartment. Richard came behind me and closed the door.

"Why you are here Richard?"

"I don't know Sophie."

"If you don't know, Richard, it's better for you to leave right now."

He sat down on the sofa. I was close to the windows overlooking the cars and shine of light outside of my apartment. In this moment I could breathe good. I was with less pain than before. Just to see him in my apartment made me calm down for a while.

"Sophie, I don't know what to say."

I turned my face to him. His eyes turned to the floor, his hands were together and he was nervous.

"Just answer me this question, Richard: Why you never told me that you were married?"

In this moment, we look to each other. He tries keeping looking at me, but he turned his face...

"Sophie, at first, I never imagined that you and I could have any relationship. Second, I thought you knew that I was married. Everybody in the office knows that I am married."

"You are a fucking liar Richard!!!"

"Sophie, when we were involved more than I thought, I realized that you didn't know about my life at all... And I don't want to lose you, I was scared to tell you the truth and you could leave me..."

When he told me about it, I could not control myself. I start slapped him. I slapped his face, his chest... I wanted to kill him...

"You are disgusting Richard! I hate you so much!!!"

He held my arms and made me sit down on the sofa. I started to cry. I could not stop to cry...

"Please, Sophie, forgive me..."

"Does Alison know about us?"

When I asked it to him, he stood up and walked away from me.

"No, she did not know about us Sophie. And I hope our relationship will stay in secret."

"So, you have a plan to divorce her?"

"Sophie, I am a married man. What happened between us was wrong, I should've avoided it the first time. But I could not…"

"So, Richard, you just use me to fuck, because your wife, probably doesn't fuck you?"

"Sophie, let's leave my wife outside of this conversation, please."

When I saw Richard defend his wife and being against me or my words, I understand what was happening there. I took a deep breath, and I asked him:

"Do you want stay with me Richard?"

He took a while to answer me:

"Sophie, I am sorry, but I love my wife and what we did was a big mistake. I was very involved with you, but now I don't want to take the risk of losing my family."

"What Richard? We did a big mistake. You are a coward of a man… you are a liar… you destroyed my life and are calling it a big mistake. You did that Richard, not me. You did this fucking big mistake."

"I am so sorry Sophie…"

"Get out of my apartment Richard! GET OUT!!!! GET OUT OF MY LIFE!!!"

When I started to scream, he just left without saying anything. He just left me with my broken heart, with all my love for him, he left me in pieces...

54 CHAPTER

Next morning, I left for Connecticut… I could not sleep, but I want to be with my family. Philip texted me asking if I was fine because I left the party early and said that I have a gift from the Company. I thanked him and I told him that Monday I will pick it up in the office.

While I was going to Connecticut, I was remembering that first time I went to NY and at the time I made so many plans for my life, for my career and who knows about love? Today, I am here, not that strong or confident about my dreams or plans anymore, but with one decision to make, and it needed to be done soon.

I will not tell my parents about what's happened, but I will probably quit my position in the office. I can't be around Richard. After our last conversation, I realize that Richard loves his wife and he doesn't want to be with me. Or if he does it will be just for sex.

The problem is that I am in love with him. I shouldn't have let this happen. I am a very professional woman and I know the worst thing that can happen is to be involved with a coworker. I know the rules and I let it happen… But, being close to Richard will be very painful to me and seeing him will bring my failure alive.

I need to step away from this mistake, but I am not moving back to Connecticut. I can reach a couple of people and try to find a new direction on my professional life.

My dad is already at home and he is doing very well. My mom is one hundred percent into my dad's recovery and she is not paying attention in nobody else right now. If I need her, I can forget about it.

Being close to my parents is very helpful to me. I feel so comfortable and secure about life and about myself. We laugh, talk about life and see my parents together bring me pain to remember if one day I could destroy some else's marriage.

I will forget Richard one day. The love that I am feeling right now is big. It can sometimes be inside my chest, and it transforms into pain, guilt, suffering and no hope for future loves.

We have a family lunch and I did not inform my family that I will quit my current job. One, because my dad would insist on me opening an office together with him, and be partners, but I am not interested in it. So, I will give time to tell them. After I quit, I will contact some friends and my old professors to find something for me.

55 CHAPTER

Monday morning, I gave my two weeks' notice letter to the Human Resources. The lady almost passed out and asked if I was sure about it and I shake my head yes. I went back to my office and I texted Philip that I need to talk to him ASAP.

I kept working on my cases, when Richard came into my office room:

"Why are you quitting?"

I keep my eyes in my files and I did not look at Richard's face. But I replied:

"Richard, I will talk to Philip about my decision. But, don't worry! I will not tell him that you are a jerk."

"Sophie, I think you are making a mistake."

"The only mistake that I did in my life, was

being involved with you, Richard. So, now I want to fix my mistakes. Being very far away from you it is the best thing that I can do right now. Please, can you leave my office. I am working."

He left my office and I looked at him. I felt much better with my decision. I think this is the smart decision that I need to do. I love this man and being around him will cause so many troubles to me...

Philip called me five minutes after Rich left my office. Philip promised to raise my salary, move for other location, other State, anything that I want, but my decision was made. No deal for right now. I thanked him so much. Working for them was one of the best things that could ever happened to me in my life, but I need to move on.

It was true. I loved working for them, but one mistake can change plans around us, change the path for a life, but I am happy with my decision. I need this time for me. I need to put myself together. At this point in my life I'm devastated. So, this moving on will be hard, but it will be healthy for me.

It is incredible how we are. I wish that Richard insisted for me to stay in the company, but he never said a word to me to stay. Maybe for him, me leaving, is of a less risk in his life... in his unfaithful life.

56 CHAPTER

I called my professor at Harvard, Mr. William, that one that offered me a job when I graduated. We talked for a while and he asked me how my career was going and how I was. I told him just about everything, besides my personal life and he enjoyed listening to me.

I ask him an opportunity to a job. It can be in London or China.

He was surprised by it, but for sure he will find something for me.

I did not tell my parents about my quit

situation yet. I want to find a job first, and then I will be informed it to them.

While I try to find a job, I start to enjoy Manhattan. I rented a bike and went to Central Park. I visited a lot of museums; I watched a lot of show in Times Square. I spend time alone, but I had so much fun in the City, every day I try different aspects of the City.

One day I was passing by in front of the W.R. Grace Building offices and I saw Richard and Philip talking... like the old days... I stop and took another direction. I don't want to meet them. I am still in love with Richard, he is the man of my life. But I am confident that I'm going to get over this love soon. I just hope it.

My professor from Harvard, Mr. William, sent me an email about one position open in England, Europe. He said I need to apply, but the position is mine, if I want to work there.

I immediately accepted the position. I needed to go. I need to enjoy my new job opportunity.

He also commented that he heard excellent feedback from Philip about my job in his company.

I told my parents my decision to move to England. My mom cries, and I told her that I need this opportunity to my career. My dad agrees with me, but he insisted about us open one office together. I told them that I was accepting the position and I will leave for Europe next week. My mom did not understand why I change the job fast like that.

"Why Sophie? You were so happy working there. Why to leave?"

Sometimes not giving an answer it is the best and smart choice in this life.

"Mom, I am young and I need new opportunities…"

57 CHAPTER

Richard texted last night, asking how I was doing. I did not answer him. Not because I don't want, it is because I don't want to bring my love alive again for him. I still love him, but in silence, waiting for it to go away...

Everyone came to say goodbye to me in the JFK Airport. Everyone from my family, I mean. It was great to me. Being support by them made me stronger and happy to move over the sea.

After the crying goodbyes, especially from my mom, I went to my gate to fly to my new life in Europe! It was exciting for me. I need the new experience for my new Sophie. Broken heart Sophie, that needed to learn from her own mistakes.

I stopped by one bookstore. I wanted to buy some magazines and books to enjoy the trip to

London. While I was looking, I saw a book titled "Secret of Marriage, by Allison Harris" ... What is this, karma?

She have all one section in the bookstore for her books. She had a lot of books. The books and his titles looks very interesting. Especially, the "Secret of marriage" I will buy it. About, the others, I will buy all of them too.

I am curious about this woman. I want to now the Richard's wife. I want to understand and I want to know her better. This woman knows how to keep her husband around her... Richard is unfaithful, but maybe our relationship made him fall in love for his wife again.

Taking my flight to London gave me a sensation, the opportunity to believe in love again, to be free of pain...

Be free from someone that I could not have forever. I am giving myself a chance to be happy again. I am giving to my heart a chance to be alive again.

I want the chance to be in love for someone again...

If you enjoy this book, or it touched your life in some way,
I would like to hear from you.

Author: Paula Avila
paulamgavila@gmail.com
(203) 676-3899

Made in the USA
Columbia, SC
12 January 2020